EVEN PAR

HOW GOLF HELPS WOMEN GAIN THE UPPER HAND IN BUSINESS

LESLIE ANDREWS
WITH ADRIENNE WAX

PUBLISHED BY 85 BROADS

ISBN: 061558800X
ISBN 13: 9780615588001

Published by 85 Broads
www.85broads.com

For my mother.

For Lorell Remington, Pamela Bicket and
Anne McCann (our editor extraordinare),
three women without whose love and support,
none of this would be possible.

CONTENTS

Introduction i

1. Carpe Diem 1

2. Myths and Realities 11

3. The Difference between Boys and Girls 21

4. The Business Benefits of Golf 33

5. Nuts and Bolts of Getting Started 45

6. How to Get the Invite, Accept the Invite,
   and Not Make a Fool of Yourself 61

7. Word Play—The Language of Golf 85

8. The Rules of Golf (The Ones You Need
   to Know Now) 91

9. Eliminating Mental Hurdles 105

10. Top 10 Must-Knows for Business Golf 115

About the Authors 123

About the Publisher 127

Leslie Andrews Golf Programs 129

Endnotes 131

Notes 133

INTRODUCTION

While working in corporate America, both Adrienne Wax and I stood out—two of the very few women bold enough to show up at corporate golf outings to play with the guys. And play we did. I worked for many years at the very male-dominated, sports-oriented ESPN. Golf was part of the fabric of ESPN, more so than in most corporate cultures, and one eschewed golf at one's own peril. I played in every outing I could.

Throughout her career as a senior-level advertising executive, some of Adrienne's most important clients were golfers, so she took advantage of every opportunity to play golf with them. Golf proved a critical tool in building client relationships, which over time translated into client retention and new business development opportunities.

It was during these golf outings that a particular phenomenon became apparent to each of us—there were few other women anywhere in sight. While this led to each of us often winning the women's prizes for longest drive and closest to the pin (given that we were two of the very few women at each of our events), it mostly made us scratch our respective heads—and wonder, "What is going on here?" We knew how much golf helped each of us in our careers, so why hadn't our female colleagues gotten the memo? Why weren't they taking advantage of the opportunities to make contacts, interact with key decision makers, and develop relationships at these events?

The seeds for this book—and for my company—were sown at the many corporate golf outings where I was surrounded by male golfers. I realized there was an opportunity to help other women understand the benefits of business golf—and to provide the tools and motivation needed to get them engaged. Since leaving the corporate world and moving into the golf world, I have had the privilege of working with thousands of women—in finance, banking, insurance, consulting, media, law, education—and with female students at many of the leading business schools in the country. They have taught me so much about the challenges they face in getting onto the golf course—way more challenges than I dreamed of when I started my business. For many, the idea of playing golf for business was not only daunting, but also totally off their radar. Even today I hear from women golfers who attend business golf outings and *still* don't feel like they belong. Yet, of the thousands I have taught, hundreds have gone from non-golfer to novice, and many from novice to passionate golfer. I am touched by the many women who come back and say "thanks" for giving them the push they needed to get into the game—and for improving their career opportunities.

Many of their stories are reflected in this book. It was written for the scores of businesswomen who have yet to understand the power they can reap from playing golf, and for those who are already in the game—but need some additional motivation to take it to the next level. Read this book in one sitting, or in chunks whenever you get a free moment in your busy days. Carry it with you to the office and to your first golf lesson. Use it to make sure you have all the bases covered the next time you get invited to a business golf outing. Buy it for young women entering the workforce so they can get a leg up from the get-go. Or share it with your "over-forty" female colleague who continues to say no when invited to a company golf outing. It's never too late to invest in yourself—and in your career. You deserve every opportunity. Use golf to help you be your best "you."

CHAPTER ONE

CARPE DIEM

"To change one's life: Start immediately.
Do it flamboyantly. No exceptions."

WILLIAM JAMES

When I worked at ESPN, my boss played golf. My boss's boss played golf. My boss's boss's boss played golf. Luckily for me, I played golf, too.

During my time there, I had the opportunity to play in a corporate outing and was invited into a foursome with my boss, his boss, and an important client. This client was a big media buyer for an advertising agency who sat on an annual budget of hundreds of millions for sports sponsorship, which we wanted her to spend with us.

On the day of the outing, it poured. We got soaked, were freezing cold, and lost a whole lot of balls. And we had a blast. Not only through the eighteen holes, but later, too, recounting the round over cocktails and dinner. Not once did we discuss business during the entire day or evening. But as a result of our day of golf, we ended up becoming fast friends and golf buddies, and she spent lots of money with us. There was an easy and natural evolution to our relationship. And all because of golf.

Throughout my career, I continued to play in every corporate golf outing I could and to take advantage of the business opportunities they afforded. Along the way,

I couldn't help but notice how few other women were out there. And it struck me that *not* playing golf was clearly a handicap for women in the work environment.

Throughout my time in corporate America, it became clear to me while attending business golf outings that my female colleagues in large part had not grasped how helpful golf could be to their careers. It certainly provided opportunities for me—I used golf successfully throughout my business career. But I had no idea that golf—and women's exclusion from it—was part of a bigger problem. For example:

- Catalyst, a prestigious research firm dedicated to expanding opportunities for women in business, did a study[1] about women in the workplace. Among other results, the research indicated that **46% of women surveyed cited "exclusion from informal networks" as the biggest impediment to reaching their career goals.** Golf was cited as one of the primary informal networks from which women felt excluded.

- In a 2007 research study[2] among financial services workers at a large U.S. corporation, a noted expert on workplace diversity was asked, "Why is it that women are making so much educational progress, yet they're still having trouble succeeding in corporate America?" Her conclusion: informal networks.

And despite the strides women have made—getting into the workforce in greater numbers, getting into more senior positions, taking up a greater number of seats at graduate schools, and getting paid better—women still face some sobering realities:

- In jobs that pay more than $100,000, women earn just 87% of what men receive.[3]

- Women hold only 15.7% of all board seats.[4]

- Women hold only 14.7% of all executive officer positions.[5]

And what makes it worse is that many people—particularly men—think the gender-inequity problem no longer exists in corporate America. They think it's been "fixed" and it's time to move on to bigger and better things. This became clear just recently as I was sharing my plans for this book with my financial planner, a very successful, progressive, forty-something male with a couple of advanced degrees. When I mentioned some of the above statistics to him, he honestly and innocently replied, "Is there really still an issue with women in the workplace? I thought we were over that."

Well, numbers don't lie, and women clearly are underrepresented in the upper echelon of the business world.

Is golf the answer? The ultimate tool to navigate the glass labyrinth? I'm not that naïve. But is golf part of "the game" of corporate America? No question it is. And while perhaps not the key to breaking through, golf might very well be one component of navigating the glass labyrinth, the complicated maze that constitutes one's career path to business success.

So what is the "value" of golf to a woman's career?

According to a survey[7] of five hundred business-women golfers:

- 73% of businesswomen surveyed agree that playing golf has helped them develop relationships and network for business.

"A labyrinth is a more fitting image to help organizations understand and address the obstacles to women's progress. Rather than depicting just one absolute barrier at the penultimate stage of a distinguished career, a labyrinth conveys the complexity and variety of challenges that can appear along the way. Passage through a labyrinth requires persistence, awareness of one's progress, and a careful analysis of the puzzles that lie ahead."[6]

- 52% agree that golf has enhanced their risk-taking abilities.

- 50% in executive-level positions agree that being able to talk about golf enables them to be more successful.

In short, golf contributes to the social capital needed to move to the upper reaches of corporate America. It is the game that gets you in the game.

No longer can the power of golf be denied by or to women. In fact, golf is the **"new MBA."** Just as with golf, there was a time not so long ago when Ivy League MBA programs were open only to men. Times have changed. Pioneering women broke down that business school barrier in the mid-1970s, and pioneering women are breaking down the business-golf barriers even as we speak. Like an MBA, golf is no longer an option in your business repertoire. Like an MBA, golf is de rigueur for women who want not only to climb the ladder, but also to run the boardroom.

Given the importance of golf to a woman's career, what is the state of the game of golf from the businesswoman's point of view?

In a nutshell: we've come a long way baby, but boy, do we have a way to go. Consider these facts:

- Women make up 50% of the population in the United States and only 23% of all golfers—and this number has not changed in years.[8]

- Women control 80% of all household purchases—hence "control the checkbook"—yet feel underserved and intimidated in a golf retail environment.[9]

- Women quit the game at a rate that is three times that of men.

What's the problem? Why don't women stick with the game and ultimately use it to their advantage in business?

The golf industry is trying, trying, trying to cater to women. Because it is an industry that traditionally was run by men for men, the change is slow; but it is coming, nevertheless. In the past decade, the golf industry has instituted national programs such as Women's Golf Month and Golf 2.0 to specifically address the unique needs of women golfers. In addition, many local golf facilities have implemented grassroots efforts with the same goal. Hence the evolution of:

- Better, more appropriate equipment for women.

- Training and instruction geared toward the specific needs of women.

- More stylish clothing—let's admit it: it matters!

- Golf programming to accommodate the schedules of working mothers—for example, 9-hole leagues and after-school kids' programs.

- Facilities with equal access—all hours of the day, all days of the week. Going, going, hopefully soon gone are the days of the Men's (only) Grill and early morning tee times reserved just for men.

The golf industry is trying to do its part: it's making the access, the equipment, and the accoutrements better.

But that's only half the equation. The second half has to come from women and businesswomen themselves. Women need to stop denying themselves the use of golf as a business tool. The opportunity is there for the taking. Why not take it?

The fact is that many women exclude themselves from business golf for a variety of reasons, many legitimate and real:

- Lack of interest in sports and/or golf

- Limited leisure time that they prefer to commit to other activities

- Family commitments, especially child rearing

However, women also exclude themselves by throwing hurdles in front of themselves. As a result of my corporate consulting, I have come to ask the following:

✓ Why do women have such a difficult time making the transition from the lesson tee to the golf course...

✓ Why do women need to play with someone they know when they join a league, often declining the opportunity to participate, rather than play with strangers...

✓ Why do women hesitate to show up at a course as a "single," willing to be paired up with whoever's available for a game...

✓ Why do women think they have to excel at the game before they can play with colleagues, clients, or the boss...

✓ *Why do so many women still think that golf just isn't something they need in their business lives...*

...while men jump into golf with both feet and no safety net, hence enjoying the benefits of developing

key relationships with clients and bosses that help pro-
pel them to success, without a thought to any of the
roadblocks/obstacles women create for themselves?

Don't get me wrong. I am not advocating that a woman act like a man, in golf or in business. I am advocating that a woman seize every opportunity to be as successful as she wants to be, however she may define that. And that includes the opportunity to leverage golf as a business tool.

Carpe diem. And seize a 5-iron while you're at it. Not tomorrow. Today.

CHAPTER TWO

MYTHS AND REALITIES

"Myths which are believed in
tend to become true."

GEORGE ORWELL

So, if women can and should seize the opportunity to leverage golf for business success, *why don't they?* And what can they do about it?

It's impossible to attend a business golf outing without noticing a pattern: in an outing with far more than a hundred attendees, fewer than ten are women. I played in dozens of outings during my business career, and since I repeatedly noticed only a handful of women at any given golf event, I began asking my female colleagues why they didn't participate in such outings. While some said they didn't participate because they couldn't play golf, the vast majority cited, in one way or another, **intimidation and fear of embarrassment** as the deterrent to their participation. There. It's out there. Women are intimidated by golf, and fear being embarrassed on the golf course. Fair enough. But it was clear to me that plenty of the guys playing in business outings had a lot of reasons to be embarrassed—and many of them probably *were* embarrassed by their level of expertise, or lack thereof. The difference? **It didn't stop them from being out there.**

Hmm, I thought. If the men can do this, why can't the women? I needed to know more. I queried my female colleagues to tell me more about this fear of embarrassment. I was astonished to learn that golf was a mystery to them—this world of pars, birdies, and bogeys—and they feared entering this unknown world.

And here's the thing: they didn't really know what they were afraid of—lacking, as they did, any experience in golf. Women conjure up myths about golf that they begin to believe. They accept these myths about golf as realities and use those "realities" to discourage themselves from getting involved in the game—and from getting the business benefits of playing golf with clients and higher-ups.

As I began to understand the myths, it became clearer and clearer to me: ***if I believed the myths, I wouldn't play golf for business either! The myths are scary!***

But here's the deal: the myths are scary. The realities are not.

It was then I realized I had found my calling—to debunk those myths and teach women the true realities of golf. Because as the old saying goes, the truth will set you free.

So let's dive in. Exactly what are the myths that keep women away from the game?

Myth #1:

To play in a business outing, you need to be a good golfer.

Reality #1:

To play in a business outing, you need to show up.

Companies run business golf outings for many reasons: to entertain clients, to reward employees, to meet new business or employment prospects, to please the golf-obsessed CEO. This list goes on and on. What the list never includes, however, is to identify the good golfers in the company (despite what the good golfers think). Golf events are run to bring people together. They're not the Olympics, and no one is expected to play like they're "going for the gold."

To play in a business golf outing, you will need:

- Courage, confidence, and a little push

- Some limited golf skills: the ability to hit the ball and get it in the air about 50% of the time

- An understanding of basic golf etiquette (more on this later): a general code of behavior about how to act on the golf course, how to keep moving forward—commonly referred to as keeping up "pace of play"—and a few basic rules (all easy to learn)

Having said you don't have to be a good golfer, I need to add that if you are in the "swing and miss" stage of your golf development (and that's OK—it's just a stage), you are not ready for a business golf outing. Not this year, anyway. You will do more harm than good to relationships if you do not have some rudimentary skills.

But, if you are in the "swing and miss" stage, you needn't be totally left out, either. Golf outings don't run themselves, they need people to run them: think PTA, charity gala, or church bake sale. You don't need to play golf—you just need to find a way to participate. Also, outings increasingly include an instructional option—perfect for a newbie. And they certainly include food and drink, so if you can eat and/or drink, you're in! Don't turn the invitation down, no matter what.

Myth #2:

All men who play in business golf outings are good golfers.

Reality #2:

Wrong. Most *people*, regardless of gender, are not good golfers. They are golfers, regardless of ability level.

A student of mine recently conveyed this story: His wife, a young, up-and-coming attorney, had been invited to her firm's golf outing. She was inclined to decline, thinking she was not good enough. Her husband **insisted** that she participate. What did she discover? She was better than average *and* she was far better than one of her male colleagues, who she considered her in-office "competition."

If you are wondering how good the men are who play in golf outings, ask them. Very few people will lay claim to being good golfers. Most people, in fact, will claim to be bad golfers. Even some good golfers will claim to be bad golfers because it is a phenomenon in golf that you are never as good as you want to be. Ever.

But, here's what most men have over most women, as it pertains to a golf outing:

- Most men have played sports to some degree.

- Most men own khaki pants and a golf shirt.

- Most men own a baseball hat.

So, for you women who are intimidated by the notion that the men playing in golf outings are good golfers, invest in a pair of khaki pants and a collared, golf-style shirt, then borrow a cap. Already you have caught up two-thirds of the way! And I'm not kidding (except, of course, that you will no doubt want to invest in a more stylish outfit...).

I don't discount the notion that having played sports is a leg up. I played sports growing up, so playing another sport—golf—wasn't a big deal to me. And it was immediately clear to me that while I was not a great golfer, I was good enough.

And that's all you need to be: good enough.

Myth #3:

Men don't like to play golf with women.

Reality #3:

Generally speaking, my experience has been that men like to play golf with women—for two reasons. First, generally speaking, most men like being with women, period, or as Jack Benny put it, "Give me golf clubs, fresh air, and a beautiful partner, and you can keep the clubs and the fresh air." And secondly, as more women move into influential roles in business—hence become key clients, bosses, and so forth—men need to build relationships with women just as much as vice versa. Remember: this isn't personal; it's business.

Having said that men like to play golf with women, I have to add a caveat to acknowledge the minority: men who do not like to play golf with women. I have played golf all over the country—in fact, all over the world—at hundreds of different golf courses. And a few times when put in a foursome

A senior level banker reports: "I was playing on a lovely, semiprivate course in Northern California, paired with a stogie-smoking man who insisted on calling me 'honey' all day long. When I asked him to stop, he replied, 'It's OK, honey; I call all my cocktail waitresses honey.'"

with men, I've received a sideward glance that said, "I really don't want to play with you." In fact, one time I observed a man specifically walking over to a starter, requesting and then being moved to a different group. And you know what? His loss and his problem. Women need to be out there to develop business relationships, and no man's discomfort should dissuade women from playing.

I will also say that no one wants to play with women (or other men, for that matter) who don't know how to act on the golf course. Develop some rudimentary skills, learn the basic etiquette, and the men will be welcoming you to the next outing.

Myth #4:

You need to make a major commitment—both in time and money—to learn to play golf and participate in golf outings for business.

Reality #4:

Golf is an investment—an investment in you. If you are moving your way up the ladder, chances are you have invested in an education, you have invested in job-specific training, you have invested in appropriate attire. Golf is just one more investment in yourself, one more tool to propel you up the ladder of your career.

So, what exactly is the investment, and how long does it take? You need an understanding of three things to play golf:

1. Basic golf skills

2. How to maintain the pace of play throughout a round

3. Golf etiquette

Learning numbers 2 and 3 takes hours, not months or years. How long does it take to develop some basic golf skills (the ability to swing and get the ball in the air being the most critical skill)? Well, it depends. I think if you make a three-month commitment—and by commitment, I mean a commitment to instruction and practice—you will have enough skill to play golf for business. Some people pick it up faster than three months' time, some people more slowly. The important thing to note is that anyone and everyone can learn to play golf. Note I did not say *master* golf; I said *play* golf. You don't have to be good. You just have to be good enough.

And while golf isn't cheap, there are ways to manage the expense of golf: hone your skills at a less-expensive course, invest in moderately priced equipment, find a friend who wants to learn and share the cost of lessons. It's an investment in your career. The cost of *not* doing it is far higher than the cost of doing it.

Myth #5:

If you're not athletic, you won't be able to learn to play golf.

Reality #5:

Anyone can learn to play golf. Anyone. At virtually any age. I have students who have never played any sports and students from four to eighty-seven years old. Just as in learning any new skill, it takes desire, a little time, and a commitment to succeed. There are no born golfers (or skiers, or pianists). And as with other skills, while some people will excel at golf, most people will plateau at some level acceptable to them—enough to enable them to enjoy it.

And that's good enough.

CHAPTER THREE

THE DIFFERENCE BETWEEN BOYS AND GIRLS

"Women need a reason to have sex.
Men just need a place."

BILLY CRYSTAL

Let's get down to brass tacks here: what really is the difference between boys and girls? We've got pink and blue. Barbie and G.I. Joe. Dora and Diego. The differences start young and they stick for life. They exist in grade school, high school, college, and business school. They translate right into the business world, and darned if those differences don't rear up on the golf course as well.

On the face of it, one might assume that the challenge of learning to play golf is the same for men as it is for women. Not so. Granted, all new golfers need to master a certain skill set, starting with grip, stance, posture, and so forth, right on to learning a cut shot or a knockdown shot. These skills are not gender-specific and can be mastered equally well by men and women. So what is so different for women in their quest to take up the game of golf? Simply put, the psychological approach of women is far different from that of men. The mind-set of the average woman learning to play golf is, "I can't do this because I'm just not a good enough player."

I taught a woman—one of my favorite private clients—who had recently retired from a job as superintendent of schools in Westchester County. She was in fabulous shape, a fitness nut, who was taking up golf with her husband to help launch her retirement. She took a lesson every week, practiced endlessly, read books on instruction, invested in equipment, clothes, and shoes…and I could not for the life of me get her onto the golf course.

Our weekly exchange would go like this:

Me: "Susie, I really want to get you out on the golf course, so you can apply some of what you are learning and start to get some feedback from playing, and we can tailor your lessons accordingly."

Her: "I'm not ready."

Me: "Yes, you are. Trust me, I know that you are ready."

Her: "I'm not good enough. I need to be better."

Me: "You are good enough. Trust me, I know that you are good enough."

Fast forward *two years*, when Susie *finally* ventured onto the golf course:

Me: "How was it?"

Her: "I can't believe I waited this long. I was way better than most of the people out there…"

Unfortunately, Susie is not atypical. The affliction of "I'm not good enough" hits girls of all ages, from five to eighty-five, and the symptoms are universal.

Symptom #1

Boys think they are entitled to play golf if they can find their way to the golf course. Girls think they have to excel at the game before they go out on the course. I'm

here to tell you: the boys are right in this instance, without question.

I have had more women than I care to acknowledge tell me that they think they need to be as good as the people they watch on television (that would be PGA Tour and LPGA Tour professionals) before they venture onto the golf course. In other words, women are saying, "I can't play golf because I am not as good as the best players in the world."

Huh?

Name one other endeavor in your life where you expect to do something as well as the *best in the world* before you make it a hobby? Would you expect to play the piano like Elton John? To sing like Aretha Franklin? Time to recalibrate those expectations.

There is a bare minimum knowledge and skill level one should have before going out to play golf:

- You should be able to propel the ball down the fairway with some regularity, preferably in the air more often than not.

- You should have an understanding of basic etiquette, especially an understanding of how to maintain pace of play.

- You should have some clue about the rules, but not much more than a clue, because the rules of golf are endlessly complicated.

That's it. Guys get this. They understand that the real point of golf is to go out and have fun, spend the day with some buddies, hit a couple of good shots and lots of lousy shots, have a few drinks, and go home. Come back next weekend and repeat. Or just show up at the company outing and smack a few balls around for eighteen holes. As a result, men are far more likely to reap the business benefits of golf, simply because they are out there, not because they are doing a good imitation of Jack Nicklaus.

I recommend to female students who suffer from this symptom that they spend a half hour near the first tee of a golf course to observe several foursomes as they tee off. In the course of thirty minutes, you are likely to see a wide variety of shots—chances are most of them will go way right, way left, way anywhere-but-straight, and there will probably

A top real estate producer chimes in: "I thought I had to shoot par just to show up. I played with a male colleague recently, and after a few holes, he asked to borrow my pen to mark his ball. I laughed and asked, 'What are you writing on those balls—"farewell"?' I'd never seen anyone lose so many balls. I quickly realized that I am more than good enough!"

be a fair number of ground balls. Mixed in will be the occasional good shot, but the majority of golfers are hackers, which is to say, people out there hacking their way around the golf course. And that's OK. More than OK—that's golf! The exercise of watching other golfers tee off provides women with a much-needed context within which they can understand and appreciate their ability vis-à-vis the ability of others. The average golfer is nowhere near as good as the golfers you see on television, not even close.

Moral of the story: golf imitates life in that women feel they need to be "better than," just to keep up. As it pertains to golf, women need a context in which to develop reasonable expectations—the basic expectation being that you play, not that you play particularly well.

Symptom #2

Boys are driven by fear of embarrassment. Girls are driven by fear of embarrassment. This is not a typo. The difference is that boys are driven by fear of embarrassment for *one* hole. Girls are driven by fear of embarrassment for *eighteen* holes.

Almost every student I teach tells me about first-tee jitters. There is something about standing on the first tee box that triggers a sense of dread, a fear that the whole world is watching. Guess what? No one is watching, because each person is in a complete panic about *his or her* own tee shot. But the way men deal with that panic, and then the rest of the round, is markedly different from the approach women take.

Here's a typical scenario on the first tee. Let's say two female friends get randomly assigned to play with two male strangers on a Sunday afternoon at a public golf course. On the first tee, introductions transpire. "Hi, I'm Bob, this is Bill." "Hi, I'm Sue, this is Joanne."

Then the men proceed to say (to each other, to the air, kinda sorta not really to the women), some form of:

- "Just got a new driver. Haven't hit it yet, so I'll probably hit it all over the place today."

- "Took a lesson the other day and the pro got me all screwed up."

- "My shoulder is killing me from moving hundred-pound bags of cement to rebuild my basement."

The women chime in with:

- "I'm a brand new golfer; I'll try not to hold you up."

- "Don't worry, I'll pick up in the middle of the hole so I don't hold you up."

- "I'm not very good, but I promise not to get in your way."

In other words, the men are saying, "I'm generally a good player, but just in case I have an off day, I want to have my 'excuse du jour' on the record, because I really am better than I am about to demonstrate for the next eighteen holes," while the women are saying, "I'm not going to be any good, and besides, I really don't belong out here." Think of this phenomenon as *fear of embarrassment on steroids*.

What are people really saying on the first tee, regardless of gender? All of them are saying, "I am terrified of being embarrassed by this first tee shot." The difference is the men have made an excuse for an ensuing bad shot, while the women have essentially abdicated their right to be there in the first place. *Kind of a high price to pay for playing golf, don't you think?*

As I said, everybody suffers from first-tee jitters, and unfortunately, that feeling never goes away, no matter how good a player you become. Over time, you may worry less about making contact and more about keeping the ball in the fairway, but the anxiety is exactly the same. The important thing to remember is that one shot does not make a round, whether it is your first tee shot or a random shot in the middle of the round. The key is to hit a shot and then *forget it immediately*. It's over, done, and on to the next— ideally without carrying emotional baggage forward to subsequent holes, be that baggage elation or despair.

It is on this topic—the ability to move on from a bad shot—that the sexes diverge. Men, well, they hit that first shot and if it's good, they're happy. If it's bad, they're angry—but only momentarily. Regardless of the quality of their first shot, after they hit their second shot, the first shot is forgotten. Immediately and forever.

Women, alas...if the first shot is good (hurrah!) it is forgotten as soon as a poor shot is hit. If the first shot is bad, it is a dead weight dragged along for eighteen holes. If it's good, most women are just waiting to hit a poor shot, so they'll have something to focus on. It's as though they are looking for that weight to carry. Women remember poor shots; men focus on good shots. Women are holding themselves to an unreasonably high standard, far higher than the standard to which other golfers will hold them. *This is far beyond fear of embarrassment—it is, unfortunately, debilitating.*

Remember: the expectation is that you play, not that you play particularly well.

Symptom #3

Boys figure out a way to play, regardless of their ability level, even if the game they play in no way resembles the game you see on television. Girls believe they have to play "correctly," as etched in stone by the golf gods, whatever that means.

This is to say, most women believe that "I can't play golf because I'm not perfect."

A second-year student from Harvard Business School attended one of my workshops. She had a beautiful golf swing. When I asked her how long she'd been taking lessons, she said she'd been taking lessons for two years. When I asked her how long she'd been playing, she said she'd never been on a golf course because *she wasn't good enough.* When I asked her what she had done between her two years of business school, she said she advised a packaged-goods CEO on developing a distribution strategy in China. No worries about not being good enough there!

Ah, perfection. The bottomless pit of unreasonable expectations that tortures so many women. Without venturing into the world of psychoanalysis, let's just deal with this issue as it pertains to golf. No one is perfect. Not Tiger Woods. Not Annika Sorenstam. Not Jack Nicklaus. Not Arnold Palmer. **Not even close.** Let yourself off the hook, right from the get-go. You are not only not going to be perfect, you're not even going to be that good.

I will repeat that for high achievers: *you are not only not going to be perfect, you're not even going to be that good.* For a while. Now, different people improve at different rates, so you might well be pretty good, pretty quickly. But it is very important to understand that the LPGA Tour and PGA Tour professionals we all watch on television are making it look easy to excel at golf. It's not easy to excel. But it's easy enough to be good enough. And that's all you need to play golf for business.

In fact, as I often say to my students, the game we watch on television is a different game than the game played by amateur golfers on the weekend. Even within the world of professional golf, the greatest players are light-years better than the average tour player. Bobby Jones, one of the greatest golfers in history, once said about Jack Nicklaus, arguably the greatest golfer ever: "He plays a game with which I am not familiar."

So if that game is so different from the game played by average players, what is the average player to do in order to play the game?

In a phrase: cut yourself some slack. You're supposed to be having fun. **So have fun!**

Not even sure how to do that? Here are my Top Two Ways to Let Yourself Off the Emotional Hook (as long as you are not in a competition):

1. The *Rules of Golf* explicitly state, "The ball must be played as it lies..." Oh yeah? Says who? If your ball is in the rough and you don't want to hit it, kick it into the fairway and then hit it. Believe me, men do this all the time, and good for them.

2. When you play golf, you are supposed to count every stroke, including penalty strokes. In reality, if you don't want to keep score, don't keep score. Do you have any idea how long it would take to play golf if every weekend hacker played every ball into the hole strictly according to the rules? Forever—that's how long. Pick up at two times par and move on. Better for you, better for your playing partners, better for all.

As you are learning, do whatever it takes to slowly build your confidence so when you finally venture onto the course with others, you are not torturing yourself worrying about what they are thinking.

Once again, it's time to recalibrate those expectations. No one expects you to be perfect except you.

Remember: the expectation is that you play, not that you play particularly well.

CHAPTER FOUR

THE BUSINESS BENEFITS OF GOLF

"At an important point in my career, I knew I needed to be where the decision makers were...I was missing out on important discussions because I wasn't plugged into their community. I needed to get to know these guys in a better environment."

RUTH ANN MARSHALL
FORMER CEO OF MASTERCARD

To the businesswoman who takes advantage of them, golf provides myriad benefits—some obvious, some less so. And by contrast, the businesswoman who ignores golf's benefits puts herself at a decided disadvantage versus her male colleagues. What is it about golf—a funny game played with a little white ball—that **enables women to level the playing field**? "It's just a stupid game," you say. And in many ways, it is. But four hours on a golf course enables you to **learn about a person's character in ways virtually unmatched in other settings.** And you can then **use those insights to build solid business relationships** that you can use to your advantage again and again. You've given yourself every other advantage in your career—training, education, wardrobe, technology—why would you ignore such an important one?

The benefits of golf are subtle, interwoven into normal, everyday work interactions. I remember once walking into my boss's office at ESPN to drop off a report. I expected him to be in an executive committee meeting, as he usually was at that time each week. Instead, he was at his desk watching television. Not an unusual occurrence at ESPN, per se, but he was watching golf, so I knew from experience that he wasn't even pretending to work. He was just watching golf.

"Leslie, this guy is the greatest putter on Tour, Brad Faxon. You should watch him and use him as a model for your own putting stroke."

He popped up, grabbed a putter that was leaning in the corner of his office, and began to imitate Brad Faxon. Then he insisted that I do the same. We spent a solid twenty minutes in his office putting golf balls into a cup lying on the floor.

Then we went our separate ways and carried on with our respective workdays.

I never would have had that interaction with my boss if I did not play golf. It was like I belonged to a secret club—the secret club of golfers. Access to that club gave me the opportunity to talk with my boss in an informal and personal way on a daily basis, which, without a doubt, cemented our relationship forever. We shared a language and a way of communicating that, if not for golf, we otherwise would not have shared. The ability to move seamlessly between informal and formal communications with him came directly from the fact that I played golf. I never thought of *not* playing golf for business, because it was so easy—and beneficial—for me to do it.

I've heard it from women over and over again: how frustrated they are that their male colleagues take off early on a Friday afternoon—sometimes every Friday afternoon in the summer—to play a round of golf with fellow businesspeople. Or that during that round of golf, their male colleagues met the very prospect they'd been trying so hard to reel in! Or that they don't get invited to the annual golf outing because no one knows they're interested. Or that they get invited, but turn down the invitation for all the psychological reasons I've already discussed.

> A successful spirits salesperson reveals: "Why did I take up golf? I didn't want to be left behind. All the guys were out there, and I needed to be out there, too, and now I am. I still need to learn not to win, though...I haven't quite gotten that one (wink, wink)."

Why do men intuitively know (or assume) that it is OK to take Friday afternoon off to play golf "for business?" Because men understand the "unwritten rules."

Too often, **women don't understand the unwritten rules of business, and they make the mistake of focusing on doing a good job, only to discover that doing a good job may not be enough.** The unwritten rules are often the primary determinants of success: unwritten rules such as the importance of relationships built through affinity groups.[10] The relationships built through affinity groups such as golf get you in the conversation.

And what is everyone talking about? What are the benefits of playing golf for business?

An Excuse to Interact with the Big-wigs

Put simply, people who play golf, watch golf, talk about golf have a "secret language" and belong to a "secret club" that provides a means of communication that non-golfers can't access. Sound hokey? Well, it's true. And since it is widely reported that 90% of all CEOs play golf, if you get into golf, then all of a sudden you have a new way—maybe the only way—to connect to those in very high levels of an organization. Once you are "in the club," you become part of a world that might otherwise have been closed to you, and all you have to do is chase a little white ball around for a few hours at a time.

Getting in the Conversation

On any Monday morning, you might observe a bunch of guys in the office—one could be the executive vice president of your department—standing around the printer talking about the golf tournament they watched on television the day before. Instead of standing on the sidelines, how useful would it be to you if you could join the conversation? Need to watch the event on television? Not necessarily. Here's a tip: all you need to do is pick up the morning paper or check a sports website and read about it; then, when the conversation starts, you can talk about the winner just like everyone else. And no one needs to know how you learned about it. The important thing is that you're now in the conversation. One sentence is all you need.

Building Relationships

We've all heard (and learned firsthand) that business is all about the relationships you build. And there's no better way to build relationships with business colleagues than by sharing an interest and spending time together outside of the office. Golf is unique—you get to spend a day in a physically beautiful setting, playing a game, uninterrupted by cell phones and the like, while learning things about your playing partners both trivial and intimate. And when you're done, because you have shared a common interest that triggers uncommon passion, you have new and different ways to connect with those people—opening up conversations and possibilities perhaps difficult to broach otherwise. And when challenges arise in business—which inevitably happens—you can lean on the relationships built on the golf course and use the insights gained about your colleague or client to help solve the problems.

Golf—A Window on the Soul

"Eighteen holes of match or medal play will teach you more about your foe than will eighteen years of dealing with him across a desk," wrote sportswriter Grantland Rice.

How valuable would it be to you to gain insights about how willing your boss is to take risks? Or about how honest your client might be in contract negotiations? Or about whether a colleague has the confidence to present a new proposal to a prospective client? **Play a round of golf with someone, and you gain a window into their soul clearer and brighter than one you could get by going to lunch or attending meetings or having dinner.** You will learn what makes them tick, who they are, how they act under pressure, how they handle adversity. There is something about playing golf with a business colleague that shines a light on that person's core character traits and gives you a leg up on understanding who they are and how best to deal with them. Let's examine more closely how one gains insights into others' character traits on the golf course.

Honesty

Golf is considered a game of honor. (It is not played with referees, and if you break a rule of golf, you are supposed to call a penalty on yourself.) As a result, honesty often comes into play. How does it manifest itself?

- Your client turns in his score card and it says he scored 90, when it is clear to you or anyone in your foursome that 90 isn't even close.

- Your boss hits a shot behind a tree; the next thing you see is the movement of his leg, followed by the ball miraculously now lying two feet clear of the tree.

Situations like these—and they happen all the time—provide insight into the integrity of your playing partners. In fact, in a study of more than four hundred business executives, when asked whether they had ever cheated at golf, a majority of those surveyed admitted they had.[11]

Be prepared to find out that people cheat, because at some point, you will be forced into a situation where you will need to choose to participate in cheating or confront the cheater. Not an easy choice when it involves your boss or client. My advice is to inject humor into the situation. For example, if the scorekeeper for your team begins to fudge the numbers, you might say, "Hey guys, not for nothing, but how about we count every stroke today, just for chuckles?" Your teammates may or may not go for it, but you are on the record for advocating honesty.

Risk Taking

Virtually every shot taken on a golf course can be measured in terms of risk and reward. If you are hitting a shot off the tee and all you can see in front of you is short grass, then swinging away has little risk. But more often you are faced with shots where there is water off to the right or dense trees off to the left or bunkers between you and the green. The decisions people make before hitting these shots can reveal a lot about their risk profiles: whether they are willing to take them, whether they take them in situations where the reward is great—or not—or whether they always play it safe. What can you learn about the golfer who attempts to hit a ball out of a lake, as opposed to taking a penalty and hitting it on dry land? Or the person who attempts a shot with little margin for error—and little upside reward should he or she make it? You're not just out for fun when you're playing golf for business. Being observant as you play—and learning about your colleagues' risk profiles—will help you greatly when you're back in the office.

A young attorney shared this story of playing on a team with her boss: "His ball was behind a tree—no chance of moving the ball forward, with the best option a punch out backward onto the fairway. Somehow he saw a window, maybe six inches square, through the leaves in the tree that he was sure he could get through—he insisted we play his ball, bad though it looked to the rest of us. Long story short, three shots later, our team punched out backward onto the fairway."

Being a Team Player

Many business golf outings use group formats (usually scramble or best ball) rather than individual play so
that foursomes play as a team and submit a single team
score. These formats are used to promote camaraderie
on the golf course, encourage team play, focus on fun,
and help move things along (enabling players of lesser
ability—often newer golfers—to participate and not feel
uncomfortable). So what can we learn from players who
are constantly encouraging their team members each
time they take a shot, who bring a golf club over to a
teammate who is far from the cart? Conversely, what
about players who, despite the format, stay almost entirely
to themselves the entire round, who constantly bemoan
the shots that they hit and often throw a club in disgust,
who do nothing to encourage team members throughout
the day?

It won't take long for you to learn who could help you with
a group project back at the office—or who might be gunning
for your job and won't care what he or she has to do to get it.
And you would have learned that all from playing golf.

Humor

You're playing golf in a foursome with your boss. He
takes his first swing of the day and when he makes contact with the ball, the ball dribbles off the tee, traveling a
scant twenty yards on the ground. You cringe, wondering

how he's going to react to this unexpected—and potentially unnerving—event. Yet, when he turns to face you, he's laughing. And one by one, each of the other members of your foursome starts laughing along with him.

Laughter, particularly at one's own expense, and a sense of humor go a long way toward putting everyone at ease and making everyone in a golf group relax. Take yourself too seriously—throw a club or two, curse every other hole—and you'll be the one no one wants as a playing partner. Do everything you can to be a *good* playing partner—and using humor is one of the best ways to accomplish that.

Beware the Reflection

We've talked a lot about how the insights you glean about people on the golf course can be a very powerful tool to use off the golf course. But beware. Others on the golf course will be observing you as well. You want to demonstrate the traits that best represent you. So be sure to always put your best foot forward and use the experience to your advantage. Show of yourself exactly what you want others to see.

Doing Deals—Or Not

I'm sure it's not surprising to anyone that Donald Trump does deals on the golf course. And good for him. And good for you should you one day do the same. But the reality is that you

> "I've made some really good deals on the golf course that I don't think I would have made otherwise...I'm talking about major business deals that I've made on the golf course that have been very significant."
> —Donald Trump

should *not* be on the golf course with a hard sell. You should be out on the golf course to make contacts, network, build relationships, and gain insights into your business colleagues—which you can then use for your business success, however that plays out.

CHAPTER FIVE

NUTS AND BOLTS OF GETTING STARTED

"So whatever you want to do, just do it...
Making a damn fool of yourself
is absolutely essential."

GLORIA STEINEM

I learned to play golf the summer after I graduated from business school. I took the summer off in anticipation of starting a job in New York City in September, a job that I fully (and accurately) anticipated would allow me very little leisure time once I started working. Hence the need for a summer of leisure before taking the corporate plunge!

I spent the summer living in San Francisco and decided to learn to play golf. I knew absolutely nothing, and it was probably just as well because I am quite sure I wandered onto the golf course completely unprepared and no doubt accidentally antagonized everyone around me just by my own cluelessness.

I bought a set of "off the rack" men's clubs (no ladies clubs for me—I was an athlete—how insulting!). I never practiced, I didn't take lessons, and I dove right into playing every week. I don't recommend this as the process for taking up the game. Everything I did, I did wrong and eventually had to unlearn and relearn. Better to take a few "right steps" in the beginning and avoid the need for a complete "do-over." Better to ask a few questions and get a few answers as you get started.

Some FAQs about getting started in golf:

Where do I go to get started?

What kind of instruction is best for me?

What equipment do I need?

What should I wear?

And some answers!

Where Do I Go to Get Started?

As with anything in life, this depends on where you live and who you know. Most important is that the facility where you learn and (ideally) practice be convenient, so you will be inspired to invest the time needed to see improvement. Think of it like joining a gym—research shows that the more convenient the gym is to where you live and/or work, the more often you will work out. So, Google golf courses and find the golf facility closest to you.

That said, the only exception to the "convenience factor" would be if you have a family member who belongs to a private club to which you can get access, and that is "convenient enough."

There are essentially two types of golf facilities: those to which anyone can have access (public courses) and those which limit access to members (private clubs). Generally, the only way to get access to a private club is through a member of the club. Many business golf outings are held at private clubs, hosted by a member of that club.

The types of public facilities available include:

- Driving ranges: outdoor or indoor facilities where you practice hitting balls into big, open spaces. Balls are provided by the facility; clubs are often available for use or rent as well. Driving ranges may also have putting, chipping, and/or bunker practice areas.

- 9-hole executive courses: courses with nine short holes, great for learning.

- 9- or 18-hole courses: courses with nine or eighteen holes that have a mix of short and long holes.

At the end of the day, it doesn't matter *where* you get started. It matters *that* you get started.

What Kind of Instruction Is Right for Me?

Chances are you've played mini-golf (that counts too!). Or maybe you've gone to a driving range to hit a few balls. All good. But the fastest and best way to learn the game is by taking lessons from a qualified golf instructor. What is the definition of "qualified golf instructor?" Unless he or she is a golf instructor, this does not include husbands, boyfriends, significant others, friends, siblings, or parents. While these people all mean well and want to help, they, like you, are amateurs, and the tips you get from them may send you in the wrong direction—or worse, in multiple directions at once. Keep it simple by focusing on basic fundamentals and listening to *one **professional** voice* at a time. Take the time to find a qualified golf instructor who "speaks to you." Work with a golf pro, and when your friends offer to help, say, "Thanks, but I'm working with a pro, and it's hard enough to follow one person's advice."

How to Find a Good Pro

There are lots of places to look for a good golf pro, and a relationship with a golf pro is like any other relationship in your life—it's about chemistry. Sometimes it's there, and sometimes it's not. Don't settle. Keep looking for a pro with whom you have a connection. You should feel comfortable, you should look forward to your lessons, and most importantly, you should improve—if you are not getting better, don't assume it's you. If it's not working after three or four lessons, shop around.

To find a pro:

1. Start by asking for referrals from people you know who are taking golf lessons and are happy with the process.

2. If you don't know anyone who's taking lessons, contact the course or driving range nearest where you work or live and ask them to refer you to someone who works well with new women golfers.

3. When you do get a recommendation, ask about the professional's credentials. Look for someone who is accredited by the LPGA or PGA. While those aren't the only good teaching professionals, you can be assured that they have received extensive training.

You may get lucky and click with the first person you meet. Or you may need to do a little trial and error. What is critical is that you work with someone who is supportive, who talks in a language that makes sense to you, who encourages, and who *expects you to get better.* If you find that the professional is talking down to you, speaks either too technically or too simply for your taste, or you're not getting better, then move on. Finding a good pro will make your golf journey much more rewarding and enjoyable.

Private vs. Group Lessons

Some people like one-on-one instruction; some people (women in particular) like to take instruction in a group. There is no right or wrong to this—whatever works for you. Both options have benefits.

Benefits of one-on-one instruction:

- The instructor's focus will be on you and you alone.

- You will likely learn faster.

- You may feel more comfortable asking questions one-on-one.

- The lesson can be tailored to exactly what you want to learn, when you want to learn it.

Benefits of group instruction:

- You may feel more supported while learning with others.

- You will see that others struggle, too.

- The focus won't only be on you.

- It will be less expensive.

Regardless of which type of instruction you choose, starting out learning golf the proper way will get you off to a good start—and minimize bad habits.

What Kind of Equipment Do I Need?

So let's start with the equipment that's needed to play golf: golf clubs. If you've ventured into a sporting-goods store or golf facility, you may already be overwhelmed by the choices. Suggestion: don't go it alone! Go with a golfer you know, or work with your instructor to make the shopping experience easier and to make you better informed.

Golf clubs should "fit" you, just as sneakers or gloves or a blouse should fit. You wouldn't buy or borrow sneakers that are two sizes too big for you, right? Nor should you buy or borrow golf clubs that don't fit. It matters: you will enjoy more success more quickly if your equipment is appropriate for you. That doesn't mean you have to rush out and invest thousands of dollars in the latest and greatest before you even know if you like the game. You have choices. If you're working with your golf professional, he or she will lead you in the right direction, but if you venture out on your own, keep these tips in mind:

Graphite vs. Steel Shafts

The shaft is the most important part of a golf club. Most shafts are made from either steel or graphite. The bottom line: graphite is a much lighter, more flexible material, which makes swinging the club easier. Graphite-shafted clubs will be more "forgiving" if you don't hit the ball perfectly. So if you're a new golfer (unless you are *very* strong and athletic), there's almost no reason to buy or consider steel shafts.

You will most likely be selecting what most manufacturers refer to as "women's clubs" (sorry, but that's how they sell them) with graphite shafts. If you are tall (five feet six inches or taller), the standard "women's clubs" may be too short for you. Therefore, you can either get women's clubs custom fit to your height, or you can consider "senior" or soft men's graphite shafts. Don't get hung up on the labels—it doesn't matter what they are called; it matters that they are appropriate for you.

A media executive started taking golf lessons in October. For Christmas, her husband bought her a new driver—got a great deal on last year's model with an extra-stiff shaft. When she brought it to her next scheduled lesson, her pro asked about it and told her it was a great club—but not suited to her game. Fortunately, she was able to return it.

To Buy or Rent—That Is the Question

Some people, regardless of skill level, need to buy all the latest equipment before taking up a new sport or hobby. If you're one of those people (and you know who you are), by all means go shopping. But if you're the more cautious type who likes to try before buying, there are other acceptable options. As mentioned previously, the key is to get/use clubs that fit you. If you go for lessons, your instructor will provide appropriate equipment during your lessons. If, during your early instruction phase, you want to get out on a driving range or course, try to rent (or borrow) the same clubs you use in your lessons or similar ones. You might be able to borrow from a female friend or relative. Chances are their equipment will "fit" you pretty well. But if your father offers you his twenty-year-old clubs that are collecting dust in the attic, be polite and thankful but extremely clear. Just say no. Golf club technology improves at a rapid pace. Today's clubs are lighter and easier to swing and help you make more solid contact consistently—in short, they make it more fun to play because you can see progress much sooner. Those clubs in your father's attic? They are likely too heavy and stiff for you. You will want to give up in disgust because you won't improve. But, alas, in this case, it will be the equipment, not you. So stay away.

And if you're invited to your first business golf outing but haven't yet bought clubs and don't have an acceptable set to borrow for the day, then call the club where the outing will be held and ask to rent a set. The better public courses—and all private clubs—where outings tend to be held will have excellent equipment available to rent.

When You're Ready to Buy

Very soon after you get the "golf bug," you will want some clubs to call your own. You may decide to plunge in or tiptoe in, depending on your budget and level of commitment. Either way is fine.

- **The Full Monty:** When you're ready (for some people, this is immediate; for others it takes a while), you will want to invest in a "good set" of golf clubs, which can cost between hundreds and thousands of dollars. Do not do this alone! There are myriad choices, and you will want to create a set that will fit you for several years. All golf clubs can and ideally should be fit to your body type and your swing. When you are ready to invest in clubs, you will likely make a series of purchases: 1) a set of irons, 2) a driver, 3) a putter, 4) fairway woods, and 5) specialty clubs, such as wedges and hybrids. You can buy a full set that is all-inclusive, but most experienced golfers buy more a la carte. Don't get overwhelmed and don't be rushed. There are lots of choices, and you should take as much time as you want before committing. Ideally, find a place where you can test clubs before making a purchase, either on a driving range or, at the very least, into a net in a retail store.

If you're not ready to make a big commitment up-front, there are two good options to get you equipped:

- **Starter golf sets** (often found at stores like Target or large sporting-goods stores). These sets include not only all the clubs you'll need, but also the golf bag.

Priced very reasonably (about $200–$300 for the entire set), these are definitely worth considering as a first golf club purchase. But again, only buy a set with graphite shafts. These sets should serve you well until you've decided you are going to stick with the game and play regularly; then, chances are you'll want to trade up.

- **Used golf clubs.** Used golf clubs are a great way to go, since you should be able to get modern technology at a significant discount from new clubs. If you stick with one of the major manufacturers (Callaway, Cobra, Ping, Nike, among others), you will be assured of good quality. As mentioned above, always check the shaft before purchasing—buy graphite and probably a women's flex, unless you are particularly athletic, strong, or tall. Many pro shops deal in previously owned equipment, and there are many online sources of equipment. Just be sure to ask a few questions before you plunk down your credit card. Ill-fitting clubs are worse than no clubs at all.

Can I Just Buy a Few Clubs to Start?

Absolutely. While you are allowed to carry up to fourteen clubs, as a new golfer, you won't need that many. You can start and continue for a while using only four clubs: one to hit the ball off the tee, one to hit the ball in the fairway, a short iron to hit shots around the green, and a putter to knock the ball into the hole. Using the above suggestions, go to a golf retailer and ask him to sell you a driver, a 7-iron, a wedge, and a putter. However, if you don't have a golf bag in which to carry these, you may be better off buying a full set.

There are many, many resources available for you to learn about golf equipment. My goal here is to help you get started by giving you enough guidance to send you in the proper direction.

The Other Stuff

There are a few other golf-related items you'll need to play golf. These include: a golf bag for your clubs, tees, a ball-mark repair tool (to repair indentations made by a ball on the green), a ball mark (to mark your ball on the green). And golf balls. As with clubs, you can get overwhelmed by the golf ball choices. For now, here's all you need to know: find inexpensive balls and buy them in great quantity. As a newer golfer, you may find that you'll lose one or two. So you'll feel better losing inexpensive balls. As you get better, you may make different decisions. But for now, buy in bulk. You can never have enough golf balls.

What else do you need? Sunscreen (a must!). Sunglasses. A hat. Lipstick or lip gloss (again, with sun protection). Tissues. Advil (good to take before and after a round). Band-Aids. Hair brush. An emery board. A shoe horn. An umbrella. Clothes for layering (in a four- to five-hour round, weather changes can be significant, and you want to be prepared). Water and/or snacks. Money. Cell phone (only in the off or vibrate position!). And any other personal items that will make your day more enjoyable.

What Should I Wear?

Good news: golf is a shopping opportunity!

Golf. Fashion. There was a time in the not-too-distant past when these two words could not appear in the same sentence. Ah, but how things have changed. Stella McCartney. Burberry. Ralph Lauren. Donna Karan. Lacoste. These, as well as brands you've never heard of (but will come to love), all make great-looking golf clothes (and shoes!) for women. From high ticket to budget, you can get a great-looking outfit for your first business golf outing. And you should. Because half the battle is to look like you belong. So what do you absolutely need before attending your first business golf outing?

A lawyer told a story about one of her first golf outings. "I was invited by my client to his company's golf outing. While I didn't know much about golf, I knew a lot about shopping and looking good. So I went to a high-end golf retailer and told the saleswoman I needed to look great. She outfitted me from head to toe, and while most of my shots looked bad, I looked good. And I felt great being out there."

The Great Golf Outfit

Getting ready for a major presentation to a new client? The first thing you'll do the night before is make sure your best outfit is pressed and ready. Or maybe you'll even go out and buy a new one, because you know how important it is to look good—to look like someone who is to be taken seriously. The same applies on the golf course. Company golf outing. All the senior execs to be in attendance. You need a great golf outfit. How hard can that be? Pack credit card. Get to the store (or online). Shop.

But what should you be looking for? Most golf shirts are collared, either in cotton or in the new wicking materials that keep perspiration at bay. Some of the trendier professional women golfers have gone to non-collared shirts, and in some instances you can, too. However, many business golf outings take place at private country clubs. And these clubs tend to have fairly conservative dress codes, so before you buy that non-collared shirt, give the course a call and find out their dress code. You'll want to ask about bottoms as well. Always acceptable are long, or the more fashionable Capri, pants. Skorts are skirts with built-in shorts underneath. They look great and are extremely comfortable. They are also universally acceptable. Shorts are also acceptable, but depending on the course, you may only be able to wear shorts at or below your knee (definitely no short shorts). Just call ahead to be sure.

A Great Pair of Shoes

Want a pair of shoes in every color to match your outfits? Check. Want them to look as cool off the course as on? Check. Want to wear golf sandals instead of actual shoes? Check. Want them to look and feel like your comfy sneakers? Check. Just as with the clothes, there are great golf shoes to be had. Just go out and get a pair. Or two. Or three. Because while you are allowed to play golf in sneakers, if you're trying to look the part, then you want to do it from head to toe (but for that business outing, stay away from the golf sandals).

CHAPTER SIX

HOW TO GET THE INVITE, ACCEPT THE INVITE, AND NOT MAKE A FOOL OF YOURSELF

"It's good sportsmanship to not pick up lost golf balls while they are still rolling."

MARK TWAIN

Now that you are dressed and equipped and have developed some basic skills, how do you get out there? You've got to get invited, say yes, and then know how to proceed—all of which are learnable skills. At this point if you are a novice, some of the terminology and situations I am about to discuss may be unfamiliar to you. However, they are critically important to understand— and will become essential to you once you start playing golf for business.

Step One: Get the Invite

As in all business dealings, there are successful strategies and tactics you can use to get what you want, whether it's a raise, promotion, new assignment, or transfer. When women ask why they never get invited to outings, I tell them it's because they're not working hard enough to put themselves into the best position to get the invitation. Just as you strategize and prepare before asking for a raise, so should you strategize and prepare to ask for an invitation to a golf outing.

What's the secret?

a. Let People Know You're Interested

I'm sure there are people in your firm who are golfers. How do you know?

- They talk about recent rounds they've played or great shots they've hit. (On Monday mornings, the shots are always great.)

- They discuss what Tiger Woods did in the tournament (or not in the tournament) over the weekend.

- They have pictures on their desks of when they played golf with Bill Clinton (or someone of lesser renown, perhaps).

- The calendar on their wall has pictures of Pebble Beach (even if they've never been there).

- They have a golf-ball paperweight on their desk.

- On casual Friday, they wear a golf shirt with a golf-themed logo.

What do you need to do to let people know that you are a golfer? *Advertise* that you are a golfer.

- Put a golf screen saver on your computer.

- Leave a putter in your office.

- Buy a golf calendar for your bulletin board.

- Watch five minutes of golf on Sunday, so you can contribute to five minutes of conversation on Monday.

Here's the one thing I tell women in our workshops that gets the biggest chuckle—and sends them into action. While they're at the workshop, looking like golfers, I tell them to grab a golf club and three friends. Have someone else take a picture, then print and display it in their office so when the boss walks in, he'll immediately know they're into golf.

- Talk about going to the driving range (actually going to the driving range isn't a bad idea either...).

- Most importantly, if someone asks if you are a golfer, **say yes!** They are not asking if you are a good golfer or how often you play or how long you've played. That is *way* too much information to share. The answer to the question, "Do you play golf," is *yes*, plain and simple.

So, advertise.

b. Get Involved

Golf outings are all around you—you just need to poke around and find them. Then offer to help manage the events. You don't need to be in charge; you just need to help. Don't think of this as scut work. The people who run golf outings tend to belong to private clubs; they tend to be partners, not junior staff; and because of golf, they tend to have relationships throughout an organization, particularly with senior executives, because the senior folks are the golfers. So get involved.

Find the person who runs the golf outing in your company. Better yet, find out who the assistant is to whomever runs the company golf outing. Let both of them know that you play golf and that you would like to get involved in the event. Anyone who helps generally gets to play, even if you are technically not on the invitation list.

How can you help? Help shape and coordinate the guest list—this can be a thankless task, but everyone will learn your name. Offer to help stuff goody bags (someone has to do it, and it's a bonding opportunity, believe me). Or sit at a charity booth at the outing—you are guaranteed to meet everyone attending the event, be they the CEO, key clients, or important colleagues. Remember: it's about relationships, so take every opportunity to get in a position to interact with attendees.

c. Stay Connected

Golf outings come in all shapes and sizes. And the more connected you are in your company and industry, the more opportunities you'll have to participate. For example:

Here's another idea: don't wait for someone else to have a golf outing—start your own group. I had a client who did just this—he was a fanatic when it came to golf. He probably played forty rounds of golf (for business!) per year. Still wanting more, he started his own business golf group. He made arrangements with five or six of the best local golf courses around, set up outing days throughout the year, invited all his business colleagues, vendors, agencies, and so on, *and* had the blessing of his boss because he was surrounding himself with people important to his business.

• Does your company run a golf outing or support any charities? Does the charity run a golf-outing fundraiser? By virtue of your company making a donation, chances are there will be slots available.

• Are you somebody's client? Ask if they hold a golf outing.

• Do you have a key client you would like to know better? Ask if his or her company holds a golf outing.

- Do you support a particular charity? Most charities run golf outings and often need volunteers to run the event. Offer to help and/or sign up to play and put part of your annual donation toward the charity golf outing.

Here are some other ways to find business golfing events:

- Join trade organizations, women's associations.

- Look for the golf outing at the next annual conference you attend.

- Attend your college reunion.

- Join fraternal organizations.

- Participate in private-school fundraisers.

Opportunities to play "business golf" are all around you, because you never know when you'll run into someone who knows someone who can make a deal happen.

Still think you can't get invited to a golf outing? Think harder. And if they don't ask you, **ask them**.

Step Two: Accept the Invite

Pay close attention here: when someone asks if you want to play in the annual golf outing at your firm...

Say yes.

When someone asks, "Are you a golfer?"

Say yes.

When someone asks you to a charity outing...

Say yes.

Don't say no. Say yes and worry about the details (like actually playing golf!) later.

Golfers, and the ruling bodies that run golf, take their rules very seriously. There are thirty-four rules and hundreds of permutations within each rule. But in the *Rules of Golf*, even before you get to a single rule, there is a section on etiquette—so you can only imagine how seriously it is taken.

Step Three: Know How NOT to Make a Fool of Yourself

Given that for most women, fear of embarrassment is one of the deterrents to getting on the golf course, then knowing how to avoid embarrassment is Job No. 1. In golf, the best way to avoid embarrassment is to understand golf etiquette.

What is etiquette as it pertains to golf? Clearly it is not about where the fork goes in relation to the knife. But it is the way a golfer is expected to act on the course, and it establishes her as respectful of the game. *And it may be the single most important thing a businesswoman needs to know to ensure that her golf experience is a positive one. Put another way, failing to learn the basic golf etiquette could undermine all your good intentions of taking advantage of golf as the powerful business tool it can be.*

And, fair or unfair, the stakes are higher for women because there are negative stereotypes out there about women and their lack of understanding of golf etiquette. As a woman using golf for business, the notion of etiquette extends beyond the traditional tenets of golf etiquette and includes all things that will help you make a good impression on your playing partners. So for you, understanding etiquette is paramount to using golf successfully.

These are **NEED-to-knows,** *not* **NICE-to-knows!**

a. Preparing before your Round

- Call ahead to the club to confirm your tee time, dress codes, payment policies (including tipping), locker-room privileges and dining options. Dress code matters *a lot,* and certain golf clubs, particularly high-end clubs that host corporate outings, often have very strict dress codes. They might require a collared shirt, they might prohibit sleeveless shirts, they might mandate Bermuda-length shorts—you never know. How you are dressed for an outing sets your first impression, and as we all know, first impressions last forever. Call ahead and don't be surprised.

> Little things make big impressions: before you tee off at a golf outing, bring your client an extra sleeve of balls, a granola bar, and a bottle of water—even if you know she has it all.

• Ask if people plan to change clothing for whatever festivities will follow the round. Often there is a sit-down dinner, and most people shower and change into business clothes for dinner. You don't want to be wearing your sweaty golf shirt, hair pulled back in a ponytail, when your male colleagues are in jacket and tie.

• Arrive early for your round to learn the lay of the land, particularly if you are entertaining clients. They will be looking to you for the location of the locker room, where to drop off clubs, where lunch will be served. Get a mini-tour a half-hour in advance.

• Go through your golf bag (especially if it is a rental set) to make sure you have everything you need for the day. Be sure you have plenty of golf balls and tees, a ball mark, and a ball-mark repair tool. If not, stop in the pro shop and stock up. Also check with your playing partners to see if they need anything. Save everyone in your foursome the embarrassment of being unprepared on the first tee.

b. Maintaining Pace of Play

The single biggest complaint golfers have about the game of golf is that it is too slow. And **the single worst thing you can do—during a recreational round of golf or in an outing—is to hold up the pace of play**.

What is meant by "pace of play?" Pace of play is the term given to the speed at which a round of golf is played. Maintaining pace of play means being able to keep up with the group ahead of you. Think about this: A golf course has eighteen holes. Imagine that you are the second group

"It is a group's responsibility to keep up with the group in front. If it loses a clear hole and it is delaying the group behind, it should invite the group behind to play through, irrespective of the number of players in that group. Where a group has not lost a clear hole, but it is apparent that the group behind can play faster, it should invite the faster moving group to play through."[12]

out in the morning, with only the first group in front of you. By the third hole, you have lost sight of the group in front, falling a hole behind. That means the group behind you is at least one hole behind as well. Now if they fall a hole behind you, they are now two holes behind. Multiply that by eighteen holes, and the result can be a round of golf that takes five (or even more) hours rather than the expected four hours. And no one wants to be out there for that long—as much as they might enjoy golf.

To "maintain pace of play" means to play your game at the pace established by that facility—or if none is established, to keep your play to around four hours. Keep up pace of play, and everyone will enjoy playing with you.

Sadly, there is a stereotype that women in particular don't know how to keep up the pace, so again, fair or unfair, the onus will be on you to do more than your part to keep up the pace. Don't be the one to help reinforce the stereotype. You can maintain pace of play by keeping up with the group in front of you. Stay one shot behind them. Even if there are better golfers ahead of you taking fewer shots, there are things you can do to keep up:

- **Play ready golf.** Go to your ball and be ready to hit it. As long as you are not in front of or distracting someone else who is going to hit, don't wait for them to finish before going to your ball.

- **Think about your club selection before it's your turn to hit,** so when it is your turn, you just pick the club and swing. Don't wait until you get there to think about whether an iron or a wood is the best selection. If you are so new that you don't know, then don't ponder. Hit your driver off the tee and your 7-iron all the way to the green.

- **Be sure you have a second ball** with you that you can, in seconds, put down and hit if your first ball misbehaves and becomes lost.

- **Pick up your ball if you are having a horrible hole**— spare yourself and your playing partners the pain. The rule of thumb is that you should pick up at no more than two times par (e.g., on a par four you would hit no more than eight shots). However, if that's not enabling you to keep up with those in front, consider picking up more frequently.

- **Encourage others in your group to do all of the above.** It's everyone's responsibility to keep up the pace of play. And I can assure you, if you do, everyone will be happier—including you.

c. Using Good Etiquette: On the Course

- **Decide who's keeping score.** Somebody has to do it, but not necessarily you. If you are a newer golfer, abdicate this responsibility immediately. You have enough to think about. On the other hand, if numbers are your thing, volunteer to keep score—it gives you a reason to chat with everyone in your foursome on every hole.

- **Manage separate tee boxes.** If you are playing with men, chances are they will be playing tees farther back than yours. There could be ten or a hundred yards between the tees your male playing partners are using and the tees you are using. It doesn't matter, *except* that the time spent walking between shots while playing golf is prime bonding time. If you are playing a different set of tees, loiter with your playing partners while they tee off, and make sure they walk with you as you tee off. You're there to build relationships, so don't let the separation of tees keep you apart.

- **Know who goes first. Who goes next. Then who goes.** This is dictated by two things—safety and pace of play. The initial order of play is determined randomly, except that players teeing off from forward tees hit after players teeing off from back tees—think safety first! After everyone has hit his or her shot off the tee, the next person to go is the person whose ball has traveled the shortest distance. Again, this promotes safety, because you never want to hit a ball if someone is standing in front of you. If everyone moves to the ball hit the shortest distance, there will be no one in front of that ball—thus no one can get hit. So the person farthest from the hole plays first, and the other players wait *behind* that person. If everyone is out of harm's way, the person to hit next should be the person who is ready—also known as "playing ready golf." This promotes pace of play. And you continue this all the way to the green.

- **Be prepared to hit your ball.** Have your club, ball, and tee ready—don't rummage through your bag while others are waiting. Keep a second ball in your pocket at all times in case your first shot goes astray and you need to hit a second ball. Everyone hits bad shots; all will be forgiven and forgotten as long as you hit another ball quickly so as not to hold up play.

- **Play your own ball**. Pet peeve number two for golfers, just behind slow play, is someone playing the wrong ball. How can that happen, you say? More easily than you think, so plan ahead. Before you tee off, you should identify your own ball to yourself and your playing partners by announcing, "I am playing a Title-ist with a red 2 on it." Ideally, you should put a personal mark on the ball as well, such as your initials. It is your responsibility to keep an eye on your ball as you play, and never take a swing at a ball in play unless you are absolutely sure it belongs to you, not to your playing partners. When in doubt, wait until everyone agrees whose ball is whose.

- **Refrain from talking or making noise while your playing partners are hitting**. This means silence—no chatting, no gum chewing, no potato-chip-bag crumpling, and above all, no cell phone sounds. It shows respect—you wouldn't talk while an important colleague was making a business presentation, would you?

- **Watch your partners' shots.** Compliment good ones; help them locate lost balls. Develop a camaraderie at the start of the round—"We're all out here to have fun"—and maintain it throughout, regardless of how well or poorly you play.

- **Clean up after yourself:**

  ○ **Replace or repair divots** (the marks you make on the fairway when you hit your ball and a piece of grass comes up with it). Don't hesitate to take a divot; it's one sign of a well-struck golf ball. Your responsibility is to repair any marks or damage you make to the course. To aid in the regrowth of the grass, either find the hunk of grass that came up with the swing and use it to cover the hole you made, or, in certain climates or clubs, repair the mark with the seed mixture attached to your cart.

○ **Rake bunkers.** Yes, bunkers are those nasty sandboxes spread throughout a golf course. After hitting your ball out of a bunker, use the rake provided (either in the bunker or on your cart) to smooth out the footprints you've left. Leave the bunker as you found it: smooth for the next player.

• **Don't hit into the group ahead of you.** Common sense would dictate that you not hit a golf ball into the group ahead of you, but there is a fine line between keeping up with the group ahead of you (a must!) and getting too close to the group ahead of you (not safe). If you're keeping up with the group in front of you, you are meeting your responsibility as a golfer. And if they're keeping up with the group in front of them, that's all you can ask. But even when that happens, there are times that you will feel you're moving too slowly, and as a result, you might start to hit shots while the group in front is too close. Some people think this is a subtle way of pushing the group in front to move faster. Believe me, if you've ever been hit with a flying golf ball, there is nothing subtle about it. When in doubt, wait. Safety is the only thing that trumps pace of play.

d. Using Good Etiquette: On the Green

- **Mark your ball.** Each player should carry something, such as a coin, to mark the ball on the green. This removes the ball from anyone's sight or line of putt.

- **Repair ball marks.** These are the marks made by a ball that hits the green on the fly, thus causing an indentation. Since greens are intended to be smooth (allowing you to putt without interference), any bumps will make putting problematic. So when you get to the green after hitting up, look for where your ball landed and use your ball-mark repair tool to push the edges of the indentation toward the middle of the mark, then use your putter to tap the ground and smooth it out.

- **Stand away from and out of sight of those putting.** When on the green, position yourself so you are not interfering with the concentration of the person putting. Pay particular attention to being in someone's peripheral vision. Give them space—literal and psychological—so they can focus fully on the task at hand.

- **Don't walk in any-one's line.** OK, I admit, this one sends some people into hysteria. I found this out one day as I tried to explain to a women's corporate group how one "owns the line" from their ball to the hole on the green. I explained that the line was sacrosanct

> "Line of putt" or "line" is the line that the player wants her ball to take after a stroke on the putting green, and includes a reasonable distance on either end/side of the line.

and that no player was allowed to walk on it (either causing damage to the surface or merely distracting a player who is lining up a putt). The group thought the golf gods had gone a little wacky on this one. But think of it this way: putting is where the game is won. And it takes concentration (and a smooth putting surface) to work your magic on a putt. Shouldn't you be able to do this without distraction? Is it that hard to ask people to walk behind your line (and you behind theirs)? Laugh all you want, but cross someone's line at your own risk.

- **Record scores (preferably honestly) after you leave the green.** Don't stay on the green any longer than necessary so that the next group can play up.

e. Using Good Etiquette: In the Cart

- When driving a cart, keep the speed modulated, use the safety brake, and make sure your passenger is safely in (or out) before moving the cart.

- Keep carts on cart paths or any area where signs indicate it's OK to drive them.

- Never drive carts on or near greens or bunkers.

- Don't drive while others are hitting shots.

f. Avoiding the Potential Minefields

- **Don't be a bad "golf colleague."** Golf is a game, and it's supposed to be fun. Yet, too many people make a day of golf into their own personal torture chamber. These golfers not only ruin the day for themselves, but also diminish the experience for their fellow golfers. Make sure you're not one of those people. Be the person everyone wants to play with again and again.

- **Keep it loose. Smile. Make a joke or two.** Be the one who makes the day fun.

- **Offer advice only if asked.** Let each person play his or her own game—unless they ask for help.

- **Encourage your playing partners.** Congratulate them when they make a good shot. Support them if they're feeling frustrated.

- **Respect your fellow golfers**. Give them plenty of space (literally and figuratively). Stay quiet while they're playing. Help them locate their balls if lost. If a playing partner is serious about the game, let him/her be serious.

- **Don't make the game too competitive**. It's a game, re-member?

g. Betting: To Bet or Not to Bet?

No sooner will you learn to play golf and make it to a business outing than you will be bombarded with numerous opportunities to bet on the game. Whether it's buying a raffle ticket, laying a wager on the winning team, or betting on every single shot you hit, you can be overwhelmed by it. And this seems to cut clearly down gender lines—men love to bet and women generally don't. This can become problematic, particularly if you are playing with a boss, subordinate, or client. Do you want to take $100 from your best client? Or someone who works for you? Does the act of betting on the game make you less likely to be the loose, supportive, encouraging partner that you want to be on the golf course?

While betting can add a certain spice to the game and be fun, if you are not comfortable betting, follow these simple tips:

- Opt out of all the betting. Simply state upfront that betting is not your thing and that you'd prefer not to participate. It may be an unpopular position, but don't feel uncomfortable taking it.

- If you feel you must participate to be part of the team, keep all wagering small. It won't matter one way or the other if you win or lose five or ten dollars.

- Suggest someone else keep track of who's winning, losing, and so on. Not knowing how the wagering is affecting the outcome will make it easier for you to concentrate on your own game.

- Keep your wagering to games of chance or charity tickets for which winning is based solely on luck—not on your skill level.

h. Keeping Score—a.k.a. Creative Accounting

Betting is not the only numbers game in golf—there's keeping score. Start at the tee box and hit a ball. Then hit continuous shots until you get the ball in the hole. Count all the times you hit the ball. Put the number on your score-card. Seems simple, right?

While most people are honest and write down six when it took six shots to get to the hole, others will not be so accurate. They may "forget" that they took two tee shots because they just didn't like the first one—and not count the extra one. Or they may have forgotten to count the "gimme" putt in their score. Or maybe they simply don't know how to keep score. Or they may have lost count of all the strokes they took on a given hole and put in a lower number. Is this simply forgetfulness, or is it creative accounting? And what should you do about it? That depends. Are you playing in a tournament for which expensive prizes will be given based on accurate scores? Or are you just out for a Friday afternoon after-work social game? Are you playing with someone with whom you do business (like a client)? Or were you paired with someone from out of town who you'll never see again?

What you choose to do will inevitably be based on the answers to these types of questions. You might overlook the extra strokes taken during the Friday afternoon round, while you might point out the ones that count toward expensive prizes. Remember: whatever you do, the game of golf is based on honesty and integrity. There are no umpires or referees in golf to monitor accuracy, scoring, and so on. There is only you and your playing partners. And what each of you does is a clear reflection of who you are and how you will act when you're back in the office. So think about that, and use that to guide your actions.

i. Using the 19th Hole Wisely

Often the favorite hole in a golf outing, the activity that takes place after the round at the 19th hole (the golf course bar) is just as important as what takes place during the round. Make sure you stay for the festivities. It is the single best time to solidify the relationships you've begun to establish by playing golf together. And all the attributes that will make you succeed on the course—looking and acting like you belong, being a good colleague—will serve you well here. Use the time to rehash great shots from the day. Laugh at the blunders you all made. And it's now the time in the day (as opposed to during your round of golf) when you can bring up a business opportunity or simply set an appointment to discuss it at a later date. Assuming the day went well, your boss or client is likely to be in a receptive mood. But be careful. A few too many at the 19th hole can spoil all the goodwill and respect you've built up throughout the day. Enjoy a drink with your colleagues—just be sure to mix in a soda or two throughout the evening.

CHAPTER SEVEN

WORD PLAY—
THE LANGUAGE
OF GOLF

"Language is wine upon the lips."

VIRGINIA WOOLF

As in any activity or industry, golf has a vernacular all its own. Knowing the terminology will not only make you more comfortable on the course but also will identify you as a "golfer" among your business colleagues. While the list of terms below is not anywhere near exhaustive, I've focused on the terms most important to your foray into business golf and, equally important, to your subsequent interactions around the foosball table or water cooler.

Back tees: The set(s) of tees farthest back on the teeing ground, often referred to as the "men's tees." They shouldn't be referred to that way; the original idea for establishing different sets of tees was to enable players of differing abilities to play together, unrelated to gender. So just refer to them as intended: the back tees.

Bunkers: Areas of sand found either on the fairway or around the green. They can be shallow or steep. Bunkers are known as "hazards" for a reason. Stay away!

Caddies: We love caddies. They are at or associated with a golf course and can be hired each round to carry your bag, find your balls, and help you read putts. And usually they know the course extremely well. They move with you from hole to hole throughout a round. In return they ask for liquid refreshments and payment for a job well done.

Fairway: The short grass beyond the tee box where the first shot is supposed to land. Size and shape varies by course. So does one's ability to land the ball on it.

Flag and flagstick: Located on each hole to indicate the location of the hole. The flag is (usually) visible from the fairway to let you know where you are going.

FORE: A critical vocabulary word. You need to yell it when you hit an errant shot to alert those who might be in its path.

Forward tees: The set

"Gimme": A freebie—a putt so close to the hole that a fellow golfer will "give it to you" on the assumption that there's no way you would miss it. Don't give them any reason to think otherwise—just pick it up and say thanks (but do add a stroke if you're keeping score, and understand that this is technically not allowable under the rules).

of tees farthest forward on the teeing ground, often referred to as the women's or ladies' tees. Again, they shouldn't be referred to that way—the original idea for establishing different sets of tees was to enable players of differing abilities to play together, unrelated to gender. So just refer to them as intended: the forward tees.

Hazard: See *bunker* above. Also, any bodies of water on the golf course. Both sand and water may be hazardous to your golf score.

Hole or cup: The place in the green where the ball is intended to go. Make every effort to put your ball *in* it at the end of each hole.

Hybrid: Hybrid golf clubs are a cross between woods and irons (see definitions of these below) that combine the benefits of both. They are alternatively called rescue clubs and for good reason: you can use them to rescue yourself from difficult situations on the golf course.

Irons: Not to be confused with the small appliance of the same name, these golf clubs have narrow heads and come in a variety of lofts; most of the clubs in your bag will be irons. They are used most often when hitting short or mid-range shots from the fairway or rough.

"Mulligan": According to the *Rules of Golf*, mulligans don't exist. According to everyone else, they do. They are "do overs," or "free shots" given to a golfer who hits a bad shot. They are often "sold" for charity at golf outings. They can be a golfer's best friend!

19ᵗʰ hole: The bar located in or around the clubhouse, used for recounting great (and not-so-great) shots of the day and connecting with colleagues and/or friends.

Out-of-bounds: The area beyond the boundaries of the course. This area is marked by white stakes. And no, that doesn't mean "surrender," just "get out."

Pace of play: Ensuring that you are keeping up with the group in front of you and not slowing everyone down. It's perhaps the single most important point of etiquette in golf—and particularly in business golf—so don't be the one who isn't doing it.

Provisional Ball: Comes into play when you hit your ball and believe it may be lost or out of bounds (if it is lost or out of bounds, you would have to return to where you hit it originally and hit a second ball). To speed up pace of play, rather than go search for it to find out if it is in fact lost or out of bounds, the provisional ball is hit from the same spot as the first one **before going to look for the first one**. If you find the first ball, you must play it. If you don't find the first ball, you play your provisional ball and take a penalty stroke.

Putting green: The circular area at the far end of each hole. It's the area where you'll find the flagstick and hole. And hopefully your ball.

Ready golf: The best way to keep up pace of play is to play ready golf. This means the person who is ready to play goes first. It means you are ready to play (with your ball and your club in hand) when it's your turn to play.

Rough: Varying lengths of higher grass that surround the fairway and green. It can be gnarly and more difficult to hit from than the fairway, so try not to spend too much time in it.

Shotgun: A type of weapon. Well, that's true, but as it relates to golf, it is a format of play often used in a business golf outing where everyone is assigned to start at a different hole on the course, and all players begin at the same time. This enables the entire group to finish at the same time for lunch, dinner, or drinks—the real reason everyone's at the outing to begin with.

Tee box or teeing ground: The flat surface at the beginning of each hole where you begin play. There are usually multiple sets of tees—indicated by colored markers—to accommodate various levels of players.

Tee time: An established time (e.g., 9:10 a.m.) when you are assigned to start play. Try to arrive a half hour before any tee time.

Woods: The woods (called that because they were at one time made from wood) are the longest clubs with the biggest, fattest heads. They are meant to be used when you have to hit the ball the farthest—such as from the tee box or from the fairway on a long hole.

CHAPTER EIGHT

THE RULES OF GOLF (The Ones You Need to Know Now)

"It's not wise to violate rules until you know how to observe them."

T.S. ELIOT

When I think of rules, I think of school: Don't put your feet on the desk. Don't talk. Obey the teacher. Simple to understand (even if you choose not to follow them). In golf, there are thirty-four rules and they are explained in a small book titled the *Rules of Golf,* also referred to as a rules book. The rules of golf are not simple to understand and, frankly, are often difficult to adhere to, even if you have the best of intentions.

What matters with the rules of golf is this: as with etiquette, your behavior as it pertains to the rules speaks volumes about the person you are. This may seem overly dramatic, and that's because it is. There is a saying in golf: "Golf is a game of honor," and it is a saying taken very, very seriously by golfers. Golf is a unique sport in that it is played without referees. It is incumbent on each golfer to police him- or herself, and to hold him- or herself up to an impeccable standard of behavior around the rules.

I left ESPN to join a dot-com, and as vice president of marketing for a company that had just received a generous infusion of venture capital, I spent a fair amount of time pursuing and being pursued by e-commerce partners. Golf opportunity! Where better to find potential partners for a fledgling affinity network?

I got invited to an outing at Winged Foot and found myself faced with a difficult and uncomfortable situation related to honesty—or more appropriately, to cheating. It was a high-end outing, the kind of event where before I hit a single shot, I and all the other guests were lavished with expensive gifts: Maui Jim sunglasses, Footjoy golf shoes, a Titleist wedge—all given to thank attendees for their donations. In addition, during lunch I noticed a prize table showing all the possible prizes participants could win. Like the gifts, the prizes were quite expensive.

The outing was structured as a team event, and almost all the prizes would be distributed based on overall team scores. However, each individual's score was added together to arrive at the final team score. I was playing with my host, a potential e-commerce partner, and we were randomly assigned to play with two other attendees. I volunteered to keep score for our foursome, and after each hole, each of the three other players in my foursome would tell me their score and I would record it. After just a few holes, I noticed that one of the people in my foursome was "forgetting" some shots—and consistently announcing a score that was a shot or two lower than the reality. *Uh oh*, I thought. Did he know what he was doing, or was he just unfamiliar with the rules, hence having trouble accurately assessing penalty strokes?

It didn't much matter why he was reporting low scores on every hole. The fact is I knew that as the team score-keeper, at the end of the round, I would be required to sign the scorecard, attesting to the accuracy of the scores we reported. In other words, by entering the wrong score for him, I was cheating on behalf of our team. After a couple of holes, I felt I had to "probe gently," which is to say, I had to confront him. While it made the rest of the round quite uncomfortable, his reported scores for the remaining holes were suddenly a stroke or two higher—but accurate. My host was, to say the least, impressed.

Having shared this story, let me say that the rules do get broken, intentionally or inadvertently, and often that is all right. How and why do the rules of golf get broken?

- They are endlessly complicated, and even the most experienced golfer can make a mistake—for example, take a drop that is two club lengths away when the rules might say only one club length.

- A player may know the rule and deliberately ignore it. Sometimes this is OK, and sometimes not, and it is very important to understand the difference.

How do you avoid making a mistake? First, carry a rules book. Second, when in doubt, *ask* someone else *before* you proceed with your next shot.

You may ask: do I need to carry a rules book as a beginner golfer? Answer: yes. Even if you just tuck it in your golf bag and never open it, it shows you are a "real" golfer. Should you be playing in a corporate outing when a rules question arises (and it will), if you can whip out a rules book, well...wow! You will impress your playing partners in ways you cannot imagine.

Very early in your golf career (even if you are the most casual of players), you will begin to care about the rules, simply because you will quickly find yourself in a position where you don't know what to do. For example, what do you do when your ball goes into a lake? The rules book has the answer. Or when you hit it into the woods and can't find it? The rules book has the answer. But you need to have a rules book with you to consult on the golf course—otherwise you won't be able to find the answer.

Don't have a rules book or, as is often the case, can't figure out the right thing to do, even after consulting the rules book? Ask your playing partners what to do. Within your foursome, either someone will know the rule, or the group can come to a consensus about what seems most logical. If you are still unsure, just do the best you can, and try to remember the exact scenario so you can ask a more experienced person after the round. Rules and their interpretation provide excellent fodder for discussions at the 19th hole or around the water cooler the next day. Don't miss the opportunity to generate or participate in a conversation about a rules situation—they're fun! Relationship building, remember?

So, when is it OK to ignore a rule deliberately and when not? And what does that choice tell you—about yourself and about your playing partners?

First and foremost, it is *never* OK to break the rules of golf when you are playing in a tournament or competition.

Having said that, the old cliché is: rules are meant to be broken, and that is as true about the rules of golf as it is about the rules of life. It is all right to "break" the rules in a couple of situations, particularly if, as a new golfer, you face a situation that is too daunting. For example:

- You are in a bunker, have taken three swings, and still can't get out. Just pick up your ball and toss it out.

- You have hit a ball out-of-bounds and are supposed to go back to where you hit your previous shot, but to do so would greatly inconvenience your foursome or hold up pace of play. Just drop a ball in what seems like a reasonable spot and carry on.

- You find yourself in deep rough, and you are not sure you can get the ball to move forward. Just pick up the ball and toss it into shorter grass.

Here's the key to "breaking" the rules on purpose, and *making it OK*: announce your intentions to your playing partners **before** you do it, so you are acknowledging that you **know** you are about to break a rule. Say something like, "I know I'm supposed to hit this over the water, but I just don't know if I can do it, so I'm going to drop my ball on the other side," or, "I'm not sure what to do from behind this boulder, so I am going to move my ball over to the side." **No one** will object to this. In fact, most experienced golfers will appreciate a newer golfer being conscientious about the rules of golf and, more importantly, about pace of play.

So when is it **not OK** to ignore a rule? Put simply, it's not OK to cheat. And by cheat, I specifically mean it is not OK to ignore a rule and then report a score for a hole or a round that you represent as legitimate when in fact it is not legitimate. Everybody fudges from time to time. It's easy to lose track of the number of strokes you take on a hole; it's easy to miscount penalty strokes. Sometimes you need to finesse your score on a hole because you lost a ball. Fudging happens, and it's all right. Deceiving and lying, now—those are not all right. Tell the truth, the whole truth, and nothing but the truth, and all will be well with your playing partners and colleagues. Deliberately lie about your score, and no one will ever forget. Did I mention that golf is a game of honor and that golfers take that notion very seriously?

Pay attention to how people treat the rules of golf, and you will gain valuable insights into their business habits and ethics. Just as importantly, pay attention to how *you* treat the rules of golf, because you are giving off signals as to your own business habits and ethics.

As a matter of practicality, in a typical round of golf, you'll most often be faced with certain rules over and over. I have listed below some of the most common rules situations that you may encounter in the course of a typical corporate outing. This is a small subset of the rules, and I strongly encourage you to invest in a copy of the *Rules of Golf* (www.USGA.org) so you are prepared for any situation that may arise.

- **Placement of the ball on the tee box:** When teeing off, your ball must be between and within two club lengths behind the tee markers—not in front of them. The penalty for teeing off outside the tee box is steep: two strokes.

- **Hitting a ball astray from the tee box:** This happens to the best of us. But if you do hit a ball from the tee box and think it may be lost, you can hit a provisional (or replacement) ball—a ball to be played if, after search, you cannot find the original one. You must announce to your playing partners that you are hitting a provisional ball before doing so. If you find your original ball, you must play it, and there is no penalty. If you do not find your original ball, you will play the provisional ball, and you must take a one-stroke penalty.

- **Hitting someone else's ball:** "What's the big deal?" you might ask. This is one of those things that irks golfers, so always mark your ball with a clearly identifiable mark (like your initials) *before* the round begins. Throughout the round, after you hit a shot, try to watch your ball until it stops rolling so you know which one is yours and so before you hit a subsequent shot, you know you are hitting your own ball. Not only do people get upset if you hit their balls, but it's a penalty under the rules. If you do hit someone else's ball, it is called hitting a "wrong ball," and you will get a penalty of two strokes and (if playing in a tournament) be disqualified if you don't correct it (by hitting your own ball) before teeing off on the next hole.

- **Hitting a ball into a water hazard:** There's some complexity here that I won't address, but these are the basics: any time your ball goes into a water hazard and you need to drop a ball outside the water hazard to proceed, you will be assessed a one-stroke penalty. If the hazard crosses the course in front of you such that you can easily get behind it, then it is a regular water hazard and will be marked by a yellow stake. Drop a new ball behind the hazard, keeping the point at which the original ball crossed the margin of the hazard between you and the hole, and no closer to the hole. If the hazard runs on either side of the course such that you can't easily get behind it, then it is a lateral water hazard and will be marked with a red stake instead of a yellow one. In this case you may drop a ball next to the hazard, within two club lengths of where the original ball crossed the margin of the hazard and no closer to the hole. In either case, you always have the option of returning to the spot where you hit the original ball and hit another ball from there. You are also allowed to hit a ball from where it lies within the hazard with no penalty—except perhaps to your ego. When in doubt ask, "Where should I drop?"

- **Hitting a ball onto a road or next to a wall:** Both roads and walls are *obstructions*, which in golf are defined as anything artificial. You may get relief from these obstructions without penalty by dropping the ball within one club length (but no closer to the hole) outside of or away from the obstruction so that you can swing your club. Unlike obstructions, *loose impediments* are natural objects such as stones, twigs, or insects. These may be removed without penalty as long as their removal does not cause the ball to move.

- **Touching the sand in a bunker before taking your swing:** Unlike on any other surface on the golf course, you may not touch your club to the sand in taking a practice shot or for any other reason. This is considered "testing the surface" and is not allowed. If you want to take a practice swing for a bunker shot, either do so outside the bunker or take the swing above the ball in the bunker. A penalty of one stroke is assessed for a breach of this rule.

- **Tending the flag:** While putting, a golfer may ask a fellow golfer to tend the flag (hold it in or just above the

In a tournament, Tiger Woods hit a shot that came to rest near a boulder that would have interfered with his swing. After confirming with a rules official that the boulder, despite its size, was considered a loose impediment, he implored the gallery to help him move it. After much shoving, pushing, and puffing, the boulder was moved out of Tiger's way. He then had a clear shot to the green. Ethical? Maybe not. Legal, as per the *Rules of Golf*? Absolutely.

hole to make it easy to see the hole). However, if a ball putted from anywhere on the green hits a flag that has not been removed, a two-shot penalty is assessed. Therefore, the flag being held by the person tending it must be removed before the ball hits it. So be sure to select someone to tend the flag who won't fall asleep on the job.

- **Play the ball as it lies:** Technically, you must play a ball as it lies, whether you like it or not. Put another way, you are not permitted to move a ball to improve its position or make it easier to hit. If you can't hit it because it is under a tree or in a bush or you just don't like where it is, you can take a one-stroke penalty under the "unplayable ball" rule and drop the ball within two club-lengths of the spot where the ball lay (no closer to the hole) so that you can hit it.

- **Moving a ball at rest:** Similar to the rule above, you are not allowed to move a ball at rest—either intentionally or accidentally—with your hand, a club, or anything else. The penalty is one stroke, and you need to return the ball to its original position.

- **Out of bounds:** The area on a golf course that is out of bounds is marked by while lines or stakes and/or fences. These usually reflect either the outer edge of the golf course property, or the property lines of a person's home. A player is not allowed to play a ball that is out of bounds and must return to the spot where the original ball was hit to hit another shot. A one-stroke penalty is assessed for this.

- **Maximum number of clubs in a bag—fourteen:** Particularly for newer golfers who may use just a few clubs when starting out, this rule will rarely be an issue. But when you get into the game and want to try out the latest clubs on the market, you might find your golf bag filling up. While your friends are not likely to care if you're just out for a fun round of golf, competitors in a tournament will feel differently. According to the rules, you are limited to a maximum of fourteen clubs. The penalty for exceeding this amount is a stiff one— two strokes per hole at which it occurs, to a maximum of four strokes.

CHAPTER NINE

ELIMINATING
MENTAL HURDLES

"Some people say I have attitude—maybe I do,
but I think you have to. You have to believe
in yourself when no one else does—that makes
you a winner right there."

VENUS WILLIAMS

The mental hurdles women must overcome in order to get onto the course and use golf for business success far exceed the physical hurdles—hurdles such as fear of embarrassment, feeling you don't belong, thinking everyone who plays golf is good, discomfort with unfamiliar surroundings. Women need to learn to step *over* the hurdles and not allow themselves to get tripped up.

The hurdles in front of women fall into two categories: those that prevent women from even getting to the golf course and those that can pop up in the middle of a round of golf.

Even getting into and onto the golf course can have its challenges. After I had begun work as a teaching professional, a client invited me to play at a very exclusive private club in Greenwich, Connecticut. I was delighted to accept the invitation since I had never played the course before.

I drove to the club; or rather, I drove past the club several times. The entrance was on a beautiful, tree-lined street and featured one of the smallest signs I have ever seen. I entered through a large stone gate, and the road to the clubhouse was unmarked. This is not unusual for a private club—generally the only people entering are members, and they know where the clubhouse is!

The bag drop was unmarked, but there was an attendant sitting there so I figured that was the right place to drop my clubs. I was wearing my golf clothing, but needed to change my shoes. The attendant informed me: don't change your shoes in the parking lot, and no spiked shoes are allowed in the clubhouse. I eventually got to the ladies' locker room and pulled myself together. I met my client in the Grill Room, where we had lunch, and of course, I was unable to pick up the tab because you can neither pay cash nor use a credit card; all charges are billed to an account—hers, of course, as the club member.

None of this was a surprise to me since I had played at many private clubs over the years, but I was taking mental notes on behalf of new golfers everywhere: how would anyone know how to navigate this world, I wondered, if they had never done it before?

Making the Leap onto the Golf Course

Intimidation and fear of embarrassment are by far the most common hurdles women face, so before you participate in your first business outing, take some steps to lower and eventually eliminate these two hurdles:

- Don't play your first round of golf with your boss or your client. This is what friends are for!

- Reach out to a friend who is a good and/or an experienced player. Ask him or her to take you out on the course once before your outing to play and to explain the nuances of maneuvering your way around the golf course. Experienced players *love* this. Golfers love the game and relish the opportunity to spread that love around. And we were all beginners once.

- Play in a weekly women's league. Not only will this give you the chance to work on your game and improve, it will also provide the added benefit of forcing you to play with strangers. The more often you do that, the easier it becomes. Remember: you are just as much a stranger to your randomly assigned playing partners as they are to you—and they are feeling similar anxiety about playing with a stranger.

- Go out very early in the morning or very late in the afternoon to play by yourself. Playing without a perceived audience will greatly reduce the pressure you feel when you are standing over the golf ball in front of other people. When you have gained confidence, invite another newbie to go out very early or very late so you can *both* benefit from the experience.

- Find a work "buddy" to include in your foursome in an upcoming business outing, and play a practice round in advance. Make a pact to be supportive and encouraging during the business outing. Often the words "nice try" are just the encouragement you need as you work your way through a round.

- Create a "safe foursome" for a business outing. There's nothing wrong with hand-picking your entire group for an outing—it decreases the stress, increases the fun, and most importantly, gets you "in the game."

- Seek out business outings that are played in a team format. In fact, most business events are structured as team competitions, most commonly referred to as a scramble or best ball. In the course of an 18-hole team competition, chances are that even the newest golfer will sink a putt or knock a chip shot close to the hole, even if it happens by accident.

A banking executive's story: "I was playing in my first outing. I was extremely nervous. Fortunately, it was a scramble, so it made it easier. Nevertheless, I was playing really badly. Then, on the fifteenth hole, my drive was used and my putt won the hole for my team. They were the only two shots of mine that counted all day, but that was enough. I was hooked."

- Not quite ready for one of those 120-person outings at a high-end private club? No problem. Start by creating a mini-outing all your own. If you have a client who is learning golf or who plays golf, suggest a trip to the driving range or a semi-private lesson. It is the shared experience of the shared passion that matters, and a lesson or a bucket of balls is a great way to start.

- Even a bucket of balls seem too daunting? No problem. Invite your golf-aholic client to a PGA Tour or LPGA Tour event if there is one in your area.

Not Dying of Embarrassment Once You Are On the Golf Course

Once you have taken the leap and decided to participate in a business golf outing, there are more potential mental hurdles to deal with in the course of a round. Don't be surprised to have these pop up, and know that there are simple tricks to dealing with anxiety-producing situations.

- **First-tee jitters.** First and foremost, *everyone* suffers from first-tee jitters, from the newest newbie to the best player in the world. So, as you step up to hit your first tee shot, don't be surprised by the anxiety that arises. Instead, feel the anxiety, then deliberately interrupt it. How is that done? Take a deep breath. Sing a song. Say something out loud just before you take the club away from the ball—anything at all that is unrelated to golf, like maybe a comment about the weather. Whistle. Think about what you had for dinner last night. Anything that breaks your train of thought as you are setting up to the ball will work. Then take your swing immediately, *before your brain has time to re-engage.*

- **"Everyone is watching me."** Truth be told, no they are not, but that is a hard sensation to shake. To decrease that anxiety, consider excusing yourself from competing—in other words, take the score out of the equation so your emphasis is on the process of hitting the shot, not on the result. For example, if you are a new golfer participating in a team event, tell the person keeping score for your group not to tell you what the score is and not to tell you when the shot you are about to try is critical. Or in a team event, try and go first whenever you can; that way, if you flub it, the other three members of the team still have a chance to hit a good shot, and you won't feel as much pressure to perform with all eyes on you. Another way to discourage people from "looking at you" is to ask for help—nothing diffuses attention like asking for attention. Say something like, "Hey, this ball is way below my feet. Anyone know how I should hit this?" You'll get tons of instantaneous advice, and the attention is shifted away from you, the advisee, to the advisor.

- **Swing and miss**. Ouch. I hate when this happens. But it does happen. I teach all my students to follow a swing and miss with a dead-serious, out-loud pronouncement of "practice swing," and an immediate redo. Everyone will laugh—at the pronouncement, not at you. If you have a particularly disastrous hole (and we all do), a funny line will often diffuse the tension—for example, "I'm getting my money's worth on this hole," or "I'm driving down my cost per swing on this hole." And remember, there's no shame in occasionally picking up the ball and moving on to the next hole.

- **Letting go of the previous shot.** This is so easy to say and so hard to do. A couple of suggestions: enforce a ten-second rule. Allow yourself to mutter and carry on about a miss—but *only* for ten seconds. Then, *force* yourself to shift your focus to the upcoming shot. Indulge, but only for ten seconds—it should be more than enough time. Or wear a rubber band around your wrist, and when you find yourself dwelling on a bad shot, snap the rubber band. The little stinging sensation should serve to break your negative train of thought and, again, shift your focus to the next shot.

Or count treetops. After a bad shot, count the number of treetops between you and the green. Or count bunkers. Or anything that will break the negative train of thought.

- **Don't keep score.** As a new/er golfer, it is not about the score—and if you do keep score, it is likely to make you feel bad. Instead, just put a checkmark in the box after you finish each hole, indicating to yourself (and others) that you're thrilled to have completed it.

- **Dealing with anger and frustration.** As a teacher, I much, much prefer anger to frustration on the golf course. Frustration can turn ugly and quickly become a spiral. When I feel frustration, I make a quick list of things that make me happy: my cat, cupcakes, the ocean, being healthy, sunshine, raindrops—anything to stop the "woe is me; I can't hit a golf shot" feeling. Anger is different. Anger can, and should, be channeled. My experience with women is that when they begin to play poorly, they react by playing tentatively. *Resist that urge with all your might.* When things go bad, be bold and swing hard. Sometimes there is nothing better for the psyche than to "grip it and rip it." Swing yourself right out of your shoes, and it just might release the anger and restore some balance to your swing.

CHAPTER TEN

TOP TEN MUST-KNOWS FOR BUSINESS GOLF

"A journey of a thousand miles
must begin with a single step."

LAO TSU

I used to keep a small set of plastic kids' golf clubs in my office, plus a handful of tennis balls. So armed, I could amuse myself when my energy would lag in the afternoon by chipping tennis balls against the wall in my office.

Sound like behavior that might be frowned upon in a corporate environment? Not a chance. One day I was chipping away—and this was not a subtle activity; the sound could be heard down the hall—and our CEO stuck his head into my office. Now mind you, on an organizational chart, I was three levels down from this man; he was not someone who was in my day-to-day work life. Nevertheless, there he was.

"Let me try," he said, reaching for the junior chipper in my hand. "I think I can chip one into the garbage can." He tried for fifteen minutes—practically broke a sweat trying to will the ball into the garbage can. He never got one in, and finally, exasperated, he handed the club back to me. "I'll be back," he promised. I would never have had a reason to interact with this man had it not been for golf.

From that day forward, whenever our paths crossed in the elevator or in the hallway at work, he would wink at me and say, "I'll be back." If you work in a business environment, be it a Fortune 500 corporation or "mom and pop" business, I don't need to tell you how valuable this kind of interaction is with the big guy. It is a career changer, and it is within your grasp if you just reach out and grab on.

Take the step. Make the investment. It's easy. Here are the Top 10 things to:

• Do

• Know

• Think about

...to help you learn to use golf for business success.

10. Don't let a lack of golf experience stand in your way.

According to a study by Catalyst, 46% of female executives cited "exclusion from informal networks"[13] as a main impediment to their ability to reach the top of an organization. And the biggest informal network is golf. Why would you let an inability to play golf stand in your way when it is relatively easy to learn? All you need to play golf are some basic skills.

9. Grab a friend—learn together.

Since starting my golf business almost ten years ago, I've learned that women overwhelmingly prefer learning with other women. Women are more likely to go with a friend to hit balls at the driving range. Women are more likely to take lessons with a friend. Women are more likely to attend an outing if they can go with a female colleague. So grab a friend and get to it. Chances are you'll enjoy it more, and you'll be more likely to stick with it.

8. Be an advanced scout and get the lay of the land.

Two of the main reasons women give for not getting involved in golf include the sense of intimidation about golf and fear of embarrassment. A visit to your local golf course will help alleviate both of these. You'll learn two critical things: how to make your way around a golf facility and that most people are average players at best, regardless of gender. Taking the time to learn this first-hand before ever going out on your own will go a long way toward allaying your fears—and getting you out "on course."

7. Be prepared.

As in the Boy Scouts, nothing leads to success quite like being prepared. If you're attending a business golf outing, call ahead to the course and find out everything you'll need to know for the day: the outing format, dress codes (for golf and afterward), whether they have clubs to rent (if you need them), and anything else that is unique to that course or event. And if you are hosting a client, ask if you can make all the financial arrangements in advance—so you can concentrate totally on being a good hostess. Don't leave anything to chance.

6. Walk the walk.

Looking the part is half the battle. Go out and get a great golf outfit and a pair of shoes to match. Make sure you have a set of clubs—yours, borrowed, or rented—as well as the accessories (golf balls, tees, ball markers, divot repair tools) that show you have what it takes to be "in the game."

5. Learn the "right way."

Take golf lessons from a professional instructor. Don't take instruction from husbands, boyfriends, significant others, siblings, or parents. Find a pro who takes you seriously, who speaks a language you can understand, and who is dedicated to making you better.

4. Learn golf etiquette dos and don'ts.

Etiquette is the way one is expected to act on the golf course. It is *the key* to feeling accepted and to being accepted. And to feeling like you belong on a golf course.

Etiquette, not playing ability, is what shows that you are, indeed, a golfer.

3. Maintain pace of play.

Maintaining pace of play means keeping up with the group playing ahead of you when you are playing golf. This is particularly important for women because there is a belief (untrue, I might add) that women slow down pace of play. So you don't want to do anything to perpetuate this untrue belief. Learn to keep up the pace of play and everyone will be happy to play with you—and you will feel that you belong.

2. Know that you don't have to be a good golfer to use golf for business—you just have to be good enough.

Playing golf for business is about building relationships. It is *not* about winning (though winning is always nice); it is *not* about demonstrating a superior level of play. It is about putting yourself in a situation to interact with key decision makers, to develop the relationships that translate off the golf course and into daily business life. By not being out there, you are depriving yourself of a valuable business tool. So regardless of your skill level, the only thing *you* should care about is being out there.

1. *"Yes, I'm a golfer."*

Say this **loud***:* *"Yes, I'm a golfer."* Let your bosses, your clients, and your colleagues know that you have every intention of being on the golf course where the action is. Say it with your attitude and your clothes and your equipment. Say it with a picture on your office desk of you at a golf course. Say it by saying yes every time you're invited to an outing. Say it by saying yes every time you're asked whether you're a golfer. Say it with confidence and conviction.

It is your right to be out there, to be making contacts, building relationships, and taking advantage of all the benefits golf affords the smart businesswoman.

Make the investment in yourself. Grab a 5-iron and carpe diem. Not tomorrow. Today.

About the Authors

Leslie Andrews

Leslie Andrews grew up in New England and graduated from Wellesley in 1982. A three-sport athlete in college, Leslie soon found a way to combine a love of sports with a successful career in marketing. She received her MBA from the Tuck School of Business at Dartmouth and spent the early part of her career in management consulting. In 1992, Leslie moved into the world of sports marketing. At NMG, a nationally renowned sports marketing agency, Leslie was instrumental in launching Nike Three For All, a pioneering grassroots program designed to help inner-city girls succeed through organized basketball. She also spearheaded the sports marketing efforts of brands such as Schick, Mennen, and others. Leslie moved on to ESPN in integrated marketing, where she led the efforts of major sponsors to leverage properties such as the X Games. Then, as Director of Marketing for ESPN.com, Leslie was among the first executives to promote ESPN online through ESPN.com.

In 2002, Leslie shifted gears and trained to become a golf teaching professional. She is now a Class A LPGA Teaching Professional—no small task for someone who took up golf at the age of thirty. She co-founded GolfingWomen and now directs all golf instruction and program development for the company. In 2009, she was recruited by the LPGA to serve as the executive director of the LPGA Teaching and Club Professionals to develop a new strategic vision and plan for the LPGA teaching division. She has now returned full time to run LeslieAndrewsGolf and GolfingWomen. She has a robust private teaching clientele in both New York City and Long Island, in addition to her GolfingWomen corporate clients. Leslie has been voted "Best of the Best" Golf Instructor twice in a survey by *Dan's Papers*, the largest newspaper in eastern Long Island—most recently in 2011.

Leslie is a sought-after speaker whose speaking engagements have included the Boston Golf Expo, Harvard Business School Women's Leadership Conference, Credit Suisse Women's Network, EWGA National Conference, and Columbia Business School Leadership Conference. Leslie has also appeared on TV segments relating to women and golf for WB-11 and ABC morning news, as well as on numerous radio talk shows on golf.

Adrienne Wax

Adrienne Wax was born and raised in New York City, the daughter of a NYC cab driver—hardly the typical beginning for a fledgling executive or a golfer! The product of an inner-city public school education, Adrienne worked her way through Lehman College, graduating at the ripe old age of twenty, and attended Baruch College for her MBA.

She joined Wunderman, a division of Y&R, as an account executive and early on was recognized as one of the Up and Comers by *Target Marketing Magazine*. Adrienne moved quickly up the ranks—becoming a Vice President before age thirty—and soon found herself running major pieces of business, including Kraft Foods, Ameritech, Pfizer, UPS, and others. Throughout her career, Adrienne took full advantage of her ability to play golf—first as a means of working her way up the corporate ladder, and ultimately as a way to build relationships with clients and prospective clients.

In 2002, Adrienne envisioned GolfingWomen with an eye toward helping other executive women learn to leverage a tool that had proven so successful in her own career. Drawing on the skills from her successful corporate career, Adrienne, along with Leslie Andrews, launched GolfingWomen. Using their contacts in the advertising and marketing worlds, they began to build their client base, starting with Draft, an advertising agency, as the inaugural client of GolfingWomen.

What began as a pursuit of passion driven by her love of golf has evolved into a highly successful business. Due largely to Adrienne's marketing expertise, the GolfingWomen client list now includes corporate clients, such as Goldman Sachs, KPMG, CSFB, Deloitte, and ICAP, and business schools, including Harvard, Yale, Wharton, Tuck, Duke, and NYU.

About the Publisher

85 Broads

85 Broads is a global women's network whose mission is to generate exceptional professional and social value for its members. Through regional network events and online at 85Broads.com, members invest their time, their intellect, and their financial capital in each other's ideas and businesses.

85 Broads was founded in 1997 as a network for current and former Goldman Sachs women who worked at **85 Broad Street**, the firm's NYC headquarters, and at other GS offices worldwide. In 2000, at the urging of women at Harvard Business School, the network was expanded to include women who were students and alumnae of the world's leading graduate business schools, irrespective of chosen career path.

In 2004, 85 Broads recognized the importance of further expanding the network to include women at the undergraduate level who were pursuing every career path imaginable. Over the next three years, campus clubs at 40 colleges in the US and abroad were created.

And in 2007, membership was extended in 85 Broads to **all amazing, trailblazing women worldwide** without regard to one's college or graduate school affiliation.

The women in 85 Broads are entrepreneurs, investment bankers, consultants, filmmakers, lawyers, educators, athletes, venture capitalists, portfolio managers, political leaders, philanthropists, doctors, engineers, artists, and scientists, in addition to women who are seeking to blaze new trails.

www.85broads.com

Leslie Andrews Golf Programs

If you are interested in finding out how you or your company can benefit from our golf programs for business-women—or just need lessons from a qualified (and I might add, excellent) pro, please go to:

www.LeslieAndrewsGolf.com
or call 866-689-8201

Endnotes

1. *Women and Men in U.S. Corporate Leadership: Same Workplace, Different Realities?* Catalyst Inc., 2004.
2. Karen Grainger, "Beyond the Old-Boy Network," *Indiana University Research and Creative Activity,* spring 2007.
3. Catherine Rampell, "Women Earn Less than Men, Especially at the Top," *New York Times,* November 16, 2009.
4. "Women's Earnings and Income," *Catalyst Quick Takes,* April 2011.
5. Ibid.
6. Alice H. Eagly and Linda L. Carli, "Women and the Labyrinth of Leadership," *Harvard Business Review,* September 1, 2007.
7. Susan Reed, "At the Top of Her Game," *Golf for Women Magazine,* January/February 2004.
8. *Women's Golf Market Report,* Golf Datatech, LLC, 2008.
9. Ibid.
10. Laura Sabattini, *Unwritten Rules: What You Don't Know Can Hurt Your Career,* Catalyst Inc., 2008.
11. "Survey of 410 Businessmen," Starwood Hotels, 2002.
12. *Rules of Golf,* United States Golf Association, 2012, p. 19.
13. Women and Men in U.S. Corporate Leadership, Catalyst.

NOTES:

Made in United States
North Haven, CT
10 May 2022

19074583R00093